Knowing & Experiencing God

KNOWING & EXPERIENCING GOD

FR.MACARIUS
(ATEF MESHREKY)

Knowing & Experiencing God

First edition 06/20/2017
Written by Fr. Macarius (Atef Meshreky)

Translated by Jeanette Arsany
Book design by Jane Park
Published by Shine International Inc.

Shine International Inc.
P.O. Box 364
Tolleson, AZ 85353
E-mail: shinebooksmedia@gmail.com
Website: www.shineinternational.org

ISBN 978-0-9971428-4-6

'But we all, with unveiled face,
beholding as in a mirror the glory of
the Lord, are being transformed into
the same image from glory to glory,
just as by the Spirit of the Lord.'

2 Corinthians 3:18

Table of Contents

Introduction

This book unfolds a deep understanding about the Holy Trinity: the Father, the Son, and the Holy Spirit. The purpose is to help the reader enter into a new dimension in Knowing God, not merely the knowledge of the mind, but the knowledge of experience. This can be achieved by getting in touch with the Person of God, as you go through the chapters of the book and enter into a deeper biblical understanding of God's revelation about Himself, both in the Old and New Testaments.

The book is divided into six parts that move gradually unfolding different dimensions of the biblical and theological revelation about the Person of the Trinity.

The opening part looks at the situation in our generation and how the Divine standards have been replaced. It looks into the cause of this, highlighting the state of God's people in relation to worship. This leads to a detailed discussion and explanation of Exodus 24. This chapter in the book of Exodus clearly reveals the different levels of worship, the conditions of entering into each of them, and the preparation necessary to move from one level to the other; highlighting the importance of ascending upwards on the mountain of worship, the mountain of fellowship with God. The question which this part discusses is: where do we stand on the mountain of worship?

Part two highlights God's ways in revealing Himself to us. This is discussed through four main areas; namely, God reveals Himself through Creation; through His Word; through circumstances of life; and through some qualities which we need to acquire. In this section, seven important qualities will be discussed; namely: *love*, *keeping the commandments*, having unceasing *spiritual hunger*, *purification and repentance*, *stillness*, *accepting sufferings* with awareness and understanding their purpose, and *faith* which is God's gift to man so that man can perceive the Person of God who is incomprehensible.

After a general overview of God's ways of revealing Himself, the book moves to a detailed discussion of God's ways in revealing Himself in the Old Testament and then in the New Testament.

Part three highlights God's ways of revealing Himself in the Old Testament where God reveals Himself through His Names. There are 16 names mentioned in the Old Testament, each unfolds a different dimension about God, the Father. All these names will be studied in details looking at the meaning, the origin, the derivations, where the name first occurred in the Old Testament, and the specific revelation about God through each name. On each occasion, God revealed Himself to His people according to their need.

Closely related to God's names are God's attributes. This section is a biblical study which highlights God's *divine attributes* and *spiritual attributes* as revealed in both Testaments with the corresponding biblical references.

In the New Testament, God reveals Himself through His Son. Therefore, the book will move to the New Testament to study how God reveals Himself through Jesus Christ.

Before discussing the Person of Christ and how He is revealed in the New Testament, part four gives an overview about God revealing Himself as the Trinity. This is a theological discussion and study about the mystery of the Holy Trinity and the relationship between the Persons (hypostases) of the Holy Trinity, according to the understanding of the early fathers of the Church. This is followed by an understanding into the meaning and implication of this mystery for our lives.

Part five provides a deep and detailed understanding of the Person of Christ, His work of salvation and His ministry as Prophet and Teacher, as High Priest and supreme Sacrifice, and as the Risen Lord and King.

Part six talks about the Person of the Holy Spirit highlighting the work of the Holy Spirit in the Church and how the work of the Spirit and the work of Christ go hand in hand. This part concludes with a discussion of the Holy Spirit and worship and how to worship *in spirit and truth*.

The book concludes with two important biblical studies: a study of the topic of the *'covenant'* because this topic is fundamental in knowing and experiencing God, and a detailed study of Psalm 119 because this Psalm highlights the attributes of God and the help and strength that come to us from His word.

Finally, this book is a collection of lectures that were delivered in a spiritual conference. These conferences or retreats have proved to help the people of God to be edified, strengthened and renewed in their cross-carrying journey, and encouraged to press on in their spiritual walk. These conferences also provide spiritual food and nourishment which are long acting. The talks include the biblical bases of the topic together with some of the writings and teaching of the early fathers of the Church to help the people of God to grow in grace, advance in the life of the spirit, and enter into the depth of the spiritual life.

Part I:

Where Do We Stand
on the Mountain of Worship?

Where Do We Stand on the Mountain of Worship?

We need to discern the spiritual situation of our days and perceive the divine economy that God wants to draw our attention to so that the spiritual scene of our generation can be altered.

Of course, it is impossible to cover the whole spiritual scene of our generation; yet, I want to refer to some important matters related to the subject of this book: *'Knowing and Experiencing God'*.

It has become so clear that there is an economy from the devil desiring to alter or change the *Divine Standards* revealed in God's Word, the Bible.

Because God, our Creator, is the source of these

standards, they are surely what suits man. They grant man to live the fullness of his humanity; they satisfy his inner being; they help him in fulfilling the reason and purpose of his existence; and they aid him in growing in his fellowship with God and those around him.

From time to time, we hear about new laws which the governments enforce on the peoples. These laws are totally new to the human mind and are a clear contradiction of God's laws and statutes.

Of course we are all familiar with some of the most famous examples of such legislations and laws; for example: abortion, same sex marriage, and other similar and associated matters that have now become laws and legislations.

The major question in this context would be:

Why is this happening now?

In other words, why is man becoming so daring in setting aside and abolishing God's standards and replacing them with human standards which totally neglect what has been set by God?

If we go back several years, we will notice that a striking change has taken place. In previous years, people sometimes rejected the divine standards and the laws and statutes set by God in the Scriptures. They did so either in a proclaimed way by becoming agnostic or atheist; or in a non-proclaimed way by inwardly refusing to obey the Word of God and live according to their own pleasures. Yet, the difference between then and now is that it is no more a *rejection* of God's standards but a *replacement*.

It is no longer a rejection. The rejection is the lack of obedience of the Word of God and His standards which are granted to us to help us in our human life.

It is a replacement. This refers to totally ignoring these standards and replacing them. Not only this, but people also dare to discuss that these standards should be rejected either because they are not suitable or because there should be no interference with man's freedom—forgetting that the One who has set these legislations is the Creator of man!

Why has this change taken place? Why is there this difference and why is this blind and unaware daring taking place?

I believe that at least one of the main reasons behind this situation is that the Church, the people of God, has lost the authority of her witness and testimony. The Church should be the light of the world amid the darkness of the evil one who desires to deceive humanity. Apostle Paul warned us of this beforehand saying:

'For we do not wrestle against flesh and blood, but against principalities, against powers, against <u>the rulers of the darkness of this age</u>, against spiritual hosts of wickedness in the heavenly places' (Ephesians 6: 12).

Looking more closely, we need to ask:

Why has the Church lost the power of her witness? Hasn't the Church continued to preach, evangelise, and send ministers? Why then is this happening?

I believe that the reason behind this is related to the form of worship of the Church, the people of God.

What does this specifically mean?

To answer this question, we need to go back to the Scriptures to see the initial picture of worship which God had set for His people. What was it like and how did they worship?

This leads us to Exodus 24. This chapter presents to us the first picture of the people of God worshipping together and encountering God.

According to scholars, spiritual matters presented

in the first five books of the Scriptures are the rules and the foundation which we should follow in our worship and in all our matters with God.

Exodus 24

God calls and invites His people to worship saying:

'Come up to the Lord, you and Aaron, Nadab and Abihu, and seventy of the elders of Israel, and worship from afar' (verse 1).

It is quite remarkable that, in God's mind, worship is an ascent, a going up: *'come up'*. Yet, we immediately see that this ascent or going up has *different levels* or *conditions*.

God says: *'Come up to the Lord, you* (Moses) *and Aaron, Nadab and Abihu, and seventy of the elders of Israel, and **worship from afar'**. And **Moses alone shall come near** the Lord, but **they shall not come near**; nor shall the people go up with him'.*

Here we see that:

- Moses is called to go up to the top of the mountain; to come near.

- The others: Aaron, Nadab and Abihu, and seventy of the elders of Israel are also called to ascend but not to the top of the mountain; not to the same level of nearness and closeness as Moses.

- The people are not to go up.

We notice that this calling to go up and worship came after the people of God came out of slavery in Egypt and crossed the Red Sea; and, as Apostle Paul puts it, they *'all were baptized into Moses in the cloud and in the sea'* (1 Corinthians 10: 2). This is equivalent to receiving the faith in Christ, in the New Testament; they became the people of God. Yet, despite getting out of slavery and crossing the sea—which is a kind of baptism, God did not call them to worship at that time. They actually continued to journey for three months until they reached Mount Sinai (Exodus 19: 1) before they came to the scene described in Exodus 24.

Doesn't this show that it seems that God was waiting for them to reach the mountain, the place of worship, before calling them to come up and worship? Worship should always be an ascent upwards. This is actually a clear reference to the state of Man who has fallen away from God and who needs to ascend towards God one more time.

We also see that when God chose a place to dwell in the midst of His people, Israel, this place was a high place—the Temple. The people used to go up to this high place during the feasts, singing the Psalms, called the *'Songs of Ascents'*. In the book of Psalms, we also read:

'Why do you fume with envy, you mountains of many peaks? This is the mountain which God desires to dwell in; yes, the Lord will dwell in it forever' (Psalm 68: 16).

In Exodus 24: 3 – 8, we read about the preparation for this kind of worship which has different levels of ascent, that is, different levels of nearness to the Lord. This preparation was through obeying the commandment (verses 3 and 4a) and offering the sacrifices. The blood of the sacrifice refers to the blood of Jesus, the Lamb of God, by which Man has been redeemed.

After this preparation, the ascent started:

'Then Moses went up, also Aaron, Nadab, and Abihu, and seventy of the elders of Israel, and they saw the God of Israel. And there was under His feet as it were a paved work of sapphire stone, and it was like the very heavens in its clarity. But on the nobles of the children of Israel He did not lay His hand. <u>So, they saw God, and they ate and drank</u>' (Exodus 24: 9 – 11).

The people were not able to ascend at all; they remained at the foot of the mountain. This was due to their lack of preparation, the lack of the purity and consecration necessary for the ascent, and the lack of even having a certain extent of preparation which would qualify them for the beginning of the ascent:

'Then the Lord came down upon Mount Sinai, on the top of the mountain. And the Lord called Moses to the top of the mountain, and Moses went up. And the Lord said to Moses, "Go down and warn the people, lest they break through to gaze at the Lord, and many of them perish. Also let the priests who come near the Lord <u>consecrate themselves</u>, lest the Lord break out against them." But Moses said to the Lord, "The people cannot come up to Mount Sinai; for You warned us, saying, 'Set bounds around the mountain and consecrate it.'" Then the Lord said to him, "Away! Get down and then come up, you and Aaron with you. But do not let the priests and the people break through to come up to the Lord, lest He break out against them." So Moses went down to the people and spoke to them' (Exodus 19: 20 – 25).

We read about the same matter in the book of Psalms:

'Who may ascend into the hill of the Lord? Or who may stand in His holy place? He who has <u>clean hands and a pure heart</u>, who has not lifted up his soul to an idol, nor sworn deceitfully. He shall receive blessing from the

Lord, and righteousness from the God of his salvation'
(Psalm 24: 3 – 5).

The ascent brings blessing and righteousness; yet, it requires a state of purity: from inside in the heart and from outside in the conduct.

The elders of Israel and their priests (the seventy elders of Israel, Aaron, Nadab and Abihu) were able to ascend to a certain level, but not to the top (Exodus 19: 20). There, they saw God; and they even ate and drank. This means that they had fellowship with God; it was the kind of fellowship which feeds and nourishes the inner depth of Man: his heart, spirit, and being.

Yet, we see another higher level of ascent. It was Moses who went up to this level. The Lord told Moses the following words:

"Come up to Me on the mountain and be there; and I will give you tablets of stone, and the law and commandments which I have written, that you may teach them." So Moses arose with his assistant Joshua, and Moses went up to the mountain of God. And he said to the elders, "Wait here for us until we come back to you. Indeed, Aaron and Hur are with you. If any man has a difficulty, let him go to them" (Exodus 24: 12 – 14).

Moses was able to ascend. He was prepared and trained for this over 40 years in the wilderness— in the divine school and the divine purification and consecration.

Then, we read the following words:

'Then Moses went up into the mountain, and a cloud covered the mountain. Now the glory of the Lord rested on Mount Sinai, and the cloud covered it six days. And on the seventh day He called to Moses out of the midst of the cloud' (Exodus 24: 15, 16).

In these verses we see true nearness and closeness to God; and that is why it takes place in the cloud! What does this mean? In fact, this is much deeper than any explanation or words can describe; yet, we can at least see that it is a kind of fellowship with God which human beings are not capable of perceiving or describing; it takes place in the cloud. This reminds us of the words of Apostle Paul where he says:

'I know a man in Christ who fourteen years ago— whether in the body I do not know, or whether out of the body I do not know, God knows—such a one was caught up to the third heaven...how he was caught up into Paradise and heard inexpressible words, which it is not lawful for a man to utter' (2 Corinthians 12: 2, 4).

We also notice that despite all the preparation of Moses over many years, he still needed a special preparation for six days before being called upwards. Then, on the seventh day, God called to him:

'Now <u>the glory of the Lord rested on Mount Sinai</u>, and the cloud covered it six days. And on the seventh day <u>He called to Moses out of the midst of the cloud</u>' (Exodus 24: 16).

This ascent and this special encounter with God which takes place in the clouds of God's glory (*'the glory of the Lord rested on Mount Sinai'*) requires a special invitation and call from God (*'He called to Moses out of the midst of the cloud'*).

Then, in verse 18, we read:

'So Moses went into the midst of the cloud and went up into the mountain. And Moses was on the mountain forty days and forty nights.'

This is a special and true closeness to God and to His throne which is very high above Man. Yet, God loves to encounter the person who humbles and sanctifies himself, realising that he will enter into the clouds of the glory of God:

'For thus says the High and Lofty One who inhabits eternity, whose name is Holy: "I dwell in the high and

holy place, with him who has a contrite and humble spirit, to revive the spirit of the humble, and to revive the heart of the contrite ones' (Isaiah 57: 15).

How great, amazing and glorious this experience is! At the same time, how awesome and fearful it is!

This experience completely transforms the whole being of the person. Didn't we see that Moses' face shone because of this encounter? This encounter was repeated afterwards (Exodus 33: 18 – 23; Exodus 34: 29; 2Corinthians 3: 7, 13). Didn't the Scriptures also testify about Moses saying: *'but since then there has not arisen in Israel a prophet like Moses, <u>whom the Lord knew face to face'</u>* (Deuteronomy 34: 10)? Aren't we in great need for such an encounter?

We are often satisfied by meeting the Lord at the foot of the mountain because we do not want to confront the pleasures of the soul, crucify our desires and passions, and be consecrated and prepared for the ascent.

Some may say: but we actually experience true encounters with the Lord and we experience His presence in our midst!

Yes, this may be true; but, let us not forget that this is because of the self-emptying of the Lord. He emptied Himself and was incarnated because of His love for man. When He sees us crippled and unable to go up to Him, He draws near us; He comes down to us! In His great humility, the Lord sees our crippled state and inability to ascend—due to the many ties which bind us to the earth, making our whole being heavy, slow, weak and not able to ascend—and so He comes down to us at the foot of the mountain to comfort, heal, restore and bless.

Yes, it is true that this happens; yet, it does not exempt us from our responsibility regarding the need to ascend and go up.

This is in fact the answer to the question that I raised at the beginning when I asked: Why has man dared to replace God's standards?

It is because the people of God have left their place as worshippers at the top of the mountain of fellowship. As a result, they ceased to destroy the darkness of the evil one through the light of God present and dwelling in their midst. Consequently, darkness and deceit increased; man became a god who took the place of God and started to set statutes and laws altering God's standards.

Ah, if the zeal of God starts to eat us up now;

If the Spirit of God stirs our desires;

*If we start to think of the ascent
on the mountain of God;*

*And if there were some individuals and then
some groups who start to ascend upwards again;*

*This will be accounted for the Church of Christ
in general.*

*By this, God's people will have a presence,
in the spirit, on the top of the mountain.*

As a result, things will change;

*And there will be restoration to
God's matters and His will.*

**There is another matter of crucial importance
in this ascent on the mountain of the fellowship
with God.**

Most of our prayers, if not all of them, are directed
towards ourselves: our needs, circumstances, problems;
and at best, towards our spiritual life. This is important
and blessed. Yet, we rarely think of God Himself; nor

do our prayers become an overwhelming desire and longing to know the Person of God.

At the top of the mountain, in the clouds of the glory of God, there is no talk of the self, the world, or the circumstances. The person is consumed in the Person of God alone. God loves this and longs for it; He calls us to know Him more and more: *'grow in the grace and knowledge of our Lord and Saviour Jesus Christ'* (2 Peter 3: 18).

This knowledge of God is full of mysteries. It truly requires a special grace that opens the mind so that the mind would receive God's revelation of Himself.

Some comments from the writings of the Church fathers on the ascent of Moses to meet God in the cloud:

- **St. Gregory of Nazianzus (4th century theologian)**

Putting himself in the place of Moses and speaking in his name, St. Gregory writes[1]:

"Now, when I (as if Moses is speaking here) go up eagerly into the Mount; or, in other words, I both eagerly long and at the same time am afraid; one through hope and the other through weakness, thus

---

1 Dumitru Staniloae, The Experience of God, p.100, 101.

entering the cloud and conversing with God."

The Saint wants to say that one may go up eagerly into the mountain; or, more accurately go up both eager and afraid: eager through hope and afraid

through weakness, he then enters into the cloud and converses with God.

The Saint continues saying that God commands:

If anyone be <u>an Aaron</u>, let him go up with me and let him stand near being ready, and remain outside the cloud.

If anyone be a <u>Nadab or Abihu</u>, or of the order of Elders, let him go up indeed, but let him stand afar off according to the degree of his purification.

If anyone be of <u>the multitude</u>, if he be altogether impure, let him not approach at all for it would be dangerous to him—but if he be at least temporarily purified, let him remain below and listen to the voice alone and the trumpet and the words of piety.

Comment:

Being cleansed from passions and having a sense of sinfulness and insufficiency are necessary conditions for this knowledge and shows that it is not intellectual negative knowledge, but it is a knowledge that comes through experience.

St. Gregory continues saying:

"It seems to me through what is perceived He attracts me to Him and to what is unperceived, He stirs up my admiration, longing, cleansing and gives divine image and then speaks with us like with His household."

Comment:

God is the source of power and light; and He also draws us always higher up into knowledge of Him and perfection of life. He is not a ceiling that puts an end to our ascent.

- ## St. Gregory of Nyssa (4ᵗʰ century)

About the same matter of ascent, St. Gregory of Nyssa writes[2]:

"Once the soul is released from its earthly attachment, it becomes light and swift for its movement upwards. The soul rises ever high; and will always make its flight yet higher, by its desire of the heavenly things 'straining ahead for what is still to come' (Philippians 3: 13). It makes its way upward without ceasing."

The soul is borne upwards by a continual thirst; and *"it prays God to show Himself to it."*

---

2 Ibid, p. 108, Life of Moses

- ## St. Dionysius the Areopagite (1st century)

Speaking about the ascent of Moses, St. Dionysius says[3]:

"The divine darkness is the 'unapproachable light'

where God is said to live!"

According to the Bible, the divine darkness refers to the clouds that surround God. His light is beyond man's ability to see, comprehend, or approach; and that is why He is in these clouds. There are many references to these clouds that surround God; for example, in Psalm 18, we read:

'He bowed the heavens also, and came down with darkness under His feet...He made darkness His secret place; His canopy around Him was dark waters and thick clouds of the skies' (Psalm 18: 9, 11).

The cloud is usually dark for the human being; it hides God who lives in unapproachable light. Because God dwells in unapproachable light (it is unapproachable for man), the clouds cover Him. These clouds are the divine darkness.

- ## St. Symeon, the New Theologian (10th century)

St. Symeon speaks about the vision of God by

---

3 Ibid, p. 112

those who are purified. He speaks of this vision of God as light that shines through all ages. Yet, it is a light above all understanding. By possessing Christ who has been formed within them, they abide near the One who shines with an unapproachable light.

His Poems[4]:

"You, Oh Christ, are the Kingdom of heaven;

You, are the Land of Promise;

Your grace, the grace of the Spirit,
will shine like the sun in all the saints;

And all will shine brightly to the degree of their faith,
their asceticism, their hope, their love, their
purification and their illumination by Your Spirit."

"Indeed You are none of these creatures,
but superior to all creatures;

For You are the cause of all creatures,
in so far as You are the Creator of all;

And that is why You are apart from them all;

---

4 Ibid, p. 113, 114

You are very lofty for our mind;

You are above all creatures;

You are invisible, inaccessible, unseizable, intangible, escaping all comprehension;

You remain without change;

You are simplicity itself; and yet You are all diversity

Our mind is totally incapable of fathoming the diversity of Your glory and the splendour of Your beauty!"

Deduction

From the above quotes and life experience of the Church fathers, we can deduce the following facts and truths:

1. God desires that we would have an experiential/ empirical knowledge of Him. This can never be achieved without drawing near Him, by ascending upwards. This ascent has no limit or point where it stops; it is limitless; the person himself is the one who limits and restricts his level of ascent.

2. Yet, based on the above experiences we can clearly see the importance of sanctification and purification as essential requirements to be prepared for this ascent. This is revealed in Exodus 24. This consecration and purification is the journey of repentance, asceticism, and stirring our spiritual desires which often get hindered by earthly preoccupations and ties.

3. However, we actually already know God; so, what does all this preparation to receive the knowledge of God mean?

There are actually **two kinds of knowledge**:

A. The first is an *intellectual knowledge* which may be accompanied by a certain degree of experiential/empirical knowledge; yet, in a limited way. It is not the empirical knowledge intended or which is received by ascending upwards towards the Lord.

B. The other kind of knowledge is not the knowledge in the sense we are familiar with, but it is an *experience*; it is even more than that: it is a *communion and unity*. It is an entrance into the clouds, into the presence of God. It is a movement and an inner stirring towards uniting with God. The person prepares himself for it; yet, it is completed by the grace of God which attracts us towards Him.

Some related theological phrases which we need to know and understand:

Theologians use two phrases related to the knowledge of God:

- **Cataphatic knowledge of God** (or positive theology)

- **Apophatic knowledge of God** (or negative theology)

The Cataphatic knowledge is positive. It uses "positive" terminology to describe or refer to God—terminology that describes or refers to what God is believed to be. In other words, it uses positive words to help us to know God; for example: God is the Creator of all things.

The Apophatic knowledge is negative. It uses "negative" terminology to indicate what it is believed God is not. For example, we say: God is <u>not</u> limited; He is <u>in</u>tangible, <u>un</u>approachable, etc., where we use the negative form because of our inability to describe Him who is indescribable; or because we cannot find enough and appropriate words that can help us describe Him, for we are limited and He is infinite.

'...how he was caught up into Paradise and heard

inexpressible words, which it is not lawful for a man to utter' (2 Corinthians 12: 4).

'...who alone has immortality, dwelling in unapproachable light, whom no man has seen or can see, to whom be honour and everlasting power. Amen' (1 Timothy 6: 16).

We can put it as follows:

Through **Cataphatic knowledge**, we only know God as the Creator and the cause that sustains the world. Through **Apophatic knowledge**, we gain a kind of direct experience of His mystical presence which surpasses the mere knowledge of Him as the Creator of the world.

When a person progresses in his spiritual life, the intellectual knowledge about God, as the Creator of the world, is completed with the direct and richer contemplation of Him.

Further clarification through the writings of the Church fathers

According to *St. Gregory of Nazianzus*, the intellectual knowledge of God which is deducted from the world is insufficient. It needs completion through higher knowledge which is the acknowledgment of His mystery.

Because of this, the fathers of the Church spoke about _two energies of the soul_:

- ○ The rational energy: through the _mind_

- ○ The perceptive energy: through the _nous_

We acquire knowledge of God through the *nous*.

The '*nous*'[5] is a certain *faculty* in the human soul which grants us perception of the Person of God. It is a spiritual perception or a spiritual reception and not an intellectual perception or reasoning.

We then express this *experience of God* through *the mind*. Through the mind, we find some possibility of describing what we directly experience through the nous.

Nous is a Greek word that is used numerously in the New Testament. It is translated as *'mind'*; yet this is not the accurate meaning of the word *'nous'*.

When these two faculties of the soul (nous and mind) work together in a parallel way, they help us to get a rather completed knowledge (according to the measure of our spiritual stature and degree of purification).

---

5 See also p.53

Some comments derived from the writings of the Church fathers:

Human beings are divided into four categories, depending on the level of their *noetic faculty* and also their *rational faculty*[6]:

a. The first category

They are those with little intellectual attainments and who rise to the highest level of noetic perfection: like spiritual monks or believers with great spiritual experience.

b. The second category

They are those with the highest intellectual attainments who fall to a low or even the lowest level of noetic imperfection: like the philosophers, scientists, and academic teachers.

c. The third category

They are those who reach both the highest intellectual attainments and noetic perfection: the great fathers of the Church.

d. The fourth category

They are those of limited intellectual ability with a hardening of the heart: the majority of people.

---

6 Met.Hierotheos, I know a Man in Christ, p.29.

Finally, we can say

The knowledge of God is empirical. This is exactly like the Sciences which we read their theories and then confirm the facts through laboratory experiments. Similarly, we hear the divine facts and truths and read them in the Scriptures; yet, we need to enter into their practical experience. *The knowledge of God is always a personal experience.*

God always was and always is and will always be a Personal God; He is an Eternal Being. He told Moses: *"I AM WHO I AM"* (Exodus 3: 14).

Summary of the patristic tradition about the knowledge of God

1. There is a natural capacity for a rational knowledge of God which is both affirmative (positive) and negative; yet, without the supernatural revelation and grace, this natural capacity can hardly be maintained.

2. Knowledge through faith which is based on supernatural revelation is **superior to** the natural knowledge from reason; it strengthens, clarifies and expands this natural knowledge.

3. Through purification from passions, knowledge that comes from faith develops into **participation**

in things communicated to us by God who is above knowledge.

4. One who has this vision or experience of God is simultaneously aware that, in His essence, God surpasses the vision or experience.

5. The noetic (apophatic) experience is equivalent to a sense of mystery that neither excludes reason nor sentiment, but it is more profound than them.

Part 2:

God's Ways to Reveal Him

God reveals Himself:

Chapter 1. Through Creation: Creating the World and Man
Chapter 2. Through His Word and Commandments
Chapter 3. Through the Circumstances of Life
Chapter 4. Through Qualities We Need to Acquire

In this part, we shall discuss each of these points in detail.

A. God and the World

Introduction

+ We cannot speak about the knowledge of God without speaking about the world, because God is the Creator of the world and the world reveals God:

'For since the creation of the world <u>His invisible attributes are clearly seen,</u> being <u>understood by the things that are made,</u> even His eternal power and Godhead, so that they are without excuse' (Romans 1: 20).

The *<u>Logos</u>* of creation Himself became the *<u>Lord/</u>*

Master (Kyrios) of history by encountering humanity in time and space; here and now!

+ God created the world for the sake of humanity. It was created as a gift for the human person. Only humans can be witnesses of the glory and goodness of God, expressed through the world which He created.

+ Human beings have a priestly vocation and responsibility by which they bring creation back to God, as a gift to God.

The world as a gift; not as a tool which can enslave

Since the world was given to humanity as a gift from God, out of His love and grace, Man should in turn learn to willingly return to the Lord His goodness towards him—as we read in Psalm 116: 12: _'What shall I return to the Lord for all his goodness to me?'_

Man possesses nothing that is his own; yet, he is granted to offer thanks to God. Thanksgiving, in itself, is an acknowledgment that God is the Giver; He is the One who owns this gift which He has granted to Man. Man should receive the gift with joy and thanksgiving, acknowledging and testifying that it is a gift which he has received and not something which he possessed. In this case, the act of thanksgiving would be an act of giving back the gift to the One who owns it. _This in_ *turn protects Man from being enslaved to the world.*

But if God is absent from this scene, man would start to use the world in a way that would make him become enslaved to the world; and it would be as though man becomes controlled by the world, by nature and the animals.

+ We have two opposite examples in this context: Adam and Christ.

Adam was deceived by the fruit that was offered to him; and so he was enslaved to its sweetness; and hence, he reaped the results: Adam ate from the fruit and fell.

On the other hand, Christ, the Second Adam, was offered the same proposal by the same source, the devil, who told Him: *'command that these stones become bread'*; yet, Jesus replied saying: *'It is written, 'Man shall not live by bread alone, but by every word that proceeds from the mouth of God'* (Matthew 4: 3, 4).

By this, Jesus associated the world (nature and its fruits) to its source and Creator, who is also His Father, the heavenly Father.

Because of this, throughout the centuries, ascetics paid great attention to maintaining the balance between viewing the fruits of nature as gifts of God that they receive with thanksgiving and joy (1 Timothy 4: 4 *'For everything created by God is good, and nothing is to be rejected if it is received with thanksgiving'*; 1 Timothy 6: 17b *'God, who richly provides us with everything to enjoy'*); and at the same time, practising their asceticism, which means exercising self-control so that they do not become enslaved to eating and drinking or become attached to earthly things.

This very act is an exercise of crucifying the self. In Galatians 5: 24, we read: *'And those who belong to Christ Jesus have crucified the flesh with its passions and desires'*. This means that one does not rely on the mere human effort but rather uses and exploits the human effort (through fasting) as a means to allow the release of the work of the Cross to the fallen nature inside him—the nature which has been enslaved to earthly matters: to *'Adam's fruit'*. By this, one would continuously live in the fullness of the freedom of redemption, *'the freedom of the glory of the children of God'*, according to Romans 8: 21b.

Providence and deification of the world

God has committed Himself to lead humans and the world into the process of deification.

The introduction of sin into the world does not

stop or obstruct the divine providence and the plan for deifying creation and the human being. This plan of deification also includes with it the redemption of mankind.

Even in the state of sin, providence preserves and directs the world. This means that the world will never be brought to utter destruction by the force of evil.

Through the constantly new and ongoing plans of the evil spirits and of the humans who are influenced by these evil spirits, evil makes every effort, aspiring to preserve itself in new forms in the world and to force its imprint deeper and deeper upon the world, in the hope of destroying it completely.

Providence, on the other hand, constantly adapts new ways to preserve and protect the world. In this, providence uses its own powers and also the good deeds of people, whether these deeds are constant or intermittent.

God constantly leads the world into new phases. Providence helps the forces of good to maintain themselves and He also helps them to obstruct and stop evil action. In leading history toward higher stages and ultimately toward salvation and deification, God makes use of both the evil and good forces. This is because providence implies synergy between God and the conscious or rational creation.

Christian teaching maintains that divine providence plays a large role in the progress of history through "new levels" which God opens up to the conscious creature. He leads creation towards these new levels and raises it up to reach them. God does not work alone; but, He works in collaboration with human action. This is because God's matters are not static; but, are dynamic, always opening up new dimensions and levels.

God does not make the existing form of the world eternal; rather, He is the God of a world which He guides and moves toward the goal of perfection in Him.

God has indeed been at work in acts of the past, and these acts moved the world forward. This is why we should believe that He works now, as well, in ways that are suitable to our own time; and that He will continue to work in the time to come in order to reveal Himself fully in the eschatological future, for it is written: *'Behold, I am making all things <u>new</u>'* (Revelation 21: 5).

This newness starts at the very beginning of our faith journey (Romans 6: 4 *'even so we also should walk in newness of life').* This means that we should walk in the new life because we have become a new creation in Jesus Christ, according to the new man which we have put on:

'Therefore, if anyone is in Christ, he is <u>a new creation</u>; old things have passed away; behold, all things have become new' (2 Corinthians 5: 17).

'For in Christ Jesus neither circumcision nor uncircumcision avails anything, but <u>a new creation'</u> (Galatians 6: 15).

'And that you put on the <u>new man</u> which was created according to God, in true righteousness and holiness' (Ephesians 4: 24).

If we continue in a living fellowship with the Holy Spirit, this newness continues through a supreme mystery. It then extends through us to the whole creation, where the mystery of newness mystically works in the whole creation as well. This mystery will be completed and manifested in its fullness in the Second Coming of Christ and the release of the power of resurrection, making everything new; where there will be a new heaven and a new earth!

'For the earnest expectation of the creation eagerly waits for the revealing of the sons of God. For the

creation was subjected to futility, not willingly, but because of Him who subjected it in hope; because the creation itself also will be delivered from the bondage of corruption into the glorious liberty of the children of God. For we know that the whole creation groans and labours with birth pangs together until now. Not only that, but we also who have the first-fruits of the Spirit, even we ourselves groan within ourselves, eagerly waiting for the adoption, the redemption of our body' (Romans 8: 19 – 23).

'Therefore, since all these things will be dissolved, what manner of persons ought you to be in holy conduct and godliness, looking for and hastening the coming of the day of God, because of which the heavens will be dissolved, being on fire, and the elements will melt with fervent heat? Nevertheless we, according to His promise, look for new heavens and a new earth in which righteousness dwells' (2 Peter 3: 11 – 13).

B. The Creation of Humanity

• The Creation of Adam

Human beings are the crown of creation, the peak of the Holy Trinity's acts of creation.

Before creating Adam, the three Persons of the Trinity took counsel together: *'Let Us make man in Our image, according to Our likeness'* (Genesis 1: 26).

This Pre-eternal Counsel of the Trinity regarding the creation of man was necessary for the following reasons:

- This was going to be a different type of creation with reason, will, and dominion over the world.

- In His Omniscience, God knew what was going to happen regarding the fall and the need for redemption.

This leads us to an important question which is ever asked and that is:

If God could foresee the fall of Adam, does this not make Adam an innocent victim?

St. John of Damascus (7th/8th century) answers this question by pointing out the distinction between 'foreknowledge' and 'predestination'. God foreknows all things but He does not predestine them.

He neither wants evil to be done ['*for God cannot be tempted by evil, nor does He Himself tempt anyone*' (James 1: 13b)], nor does He force virtue.

Sin **was not** built in Adam's nature. To sin or not to sin depended on ***Adam's free will***.

- **Image and likeness**

God created man in '*His*' own image. When the Bible speaks about human beings, it says '*created him*' and '*created them*'. This alternative use of '*him*' and '*them*' emphasises the **unity** of the nature of the human race even though each individual is **unique**.

God is *a Nature* and *three Persons*; **man** is *a nature* and *innumerable persons*.

○ *What is the image?*

The Church fathers have different views about that word '*image*'; yet, these views are all complementary.

'*Image*' is said to be:

- Intellect and reasoning
- Free will and self determination
- Creativity

- Immortality
- Virtues

In fact, *'image'* includes all these things together.

○ *What is the 'likeness'?*

If *'image'* is what has been originally fixed by the Creator, then, the *'likeness'* is that which is to be attained through the life of virtue which a person lives.

Image indicates what is reasonable and bestowed by God; while, *likeness* indicates assimilation i.e. what is received and acquired through virtue as far as it is possible.

- **Elements of the human being**

Paul speaks about three elements of the human being: spirit, soul, and body.

'Now may the God of peace Himself sanctify you completely; and may your whole <u>spirit, soul, and body</u> be preserved blameless at the coming of our Lord Jesus Christ' (1 Thessalonians 5: 23).

Yet, sometimes the Bible uses *'soul'* and *'spirit'* interchangeably.

This has led the fathers of the Church to speak about **two energies/capacities of the soul** (when the spirit is not referred to); and these are:

- ○ **Higher capacity**, *'nous'*: though *'nous'* is usually translated *'mind'*, it is different from the mind because it refers to a quality or energy that is not depending on reasoning (reasoning is the activity of the mind). It actually refers to a special energy that leads and helps the human person to come into an encounter with God as *Person to person*.

- ○ **Lower capacity** includes: imaginations, thoughts, emotions, etc.

- ▪ **The heart**

Another important word used in the Scriptures in relation to man is *'heart'*. The early Church understood this word to refer to the innermost part of the human being.

It is the centre of the spiritual and mystical life.

It is the throne of the divine presence and inner grace.

It is also understood that the mind is located in the heart (this was the case before the fall because after the fall some kind of disintegration took place between the different elements of the human being).

Dignity/honour of man (before the fall)

Man is an ***icon of the Creator***. In fact, man and angels are two different *intelligent* or *rational* creatures created for corresponding purposes.

In Psalm 8: 4 – 6, we read:

'What is man that You are mindful of him, and the son of man that You visit him? For <u>You have made him a little lower than the angels, and You have crowned him with glory and honour.</u> You have made him to have dominion over the works of Your hands; You have put all things under his feet.'

It is even believed that man is in between the angelic realm and the earthly realm; having both natures: *the intelligence of the angels* and the *material element* of the worldly creatures. Thus, it is spoken of man as ***'microcosm';*** and sometimes he is even spoken of as ***'micro-theos'***.

It is important and interesting to know that when God created the human nature, He created it, not only for us; but also, for Himself—since He knew that one day He Himself would become a human being. Thus, He fashioned something adequate for Himself, something possessing infinite potential. This is what is referred to in the writings of St. Gregory Nazianzus when he calls each person *'a created god'*!

- ### Assignments of Adam

Adam was a king, priest, and prophet.

As a king, all creatures were subdued to him and he was called by God to name them. This means that he was given an ability to know the essence of the creatures. The name reflected the purpose of existence of each creature. This act of naming the creatures is an activation of a *prophetic calling* that was granted to Adam.

Referring to Adam, St. Macarius of Egypt says: *'neither fire could overcome him, nor water drown him, nor any beast harm him.'* He also says: *'Adam's face emitted radiant glory.'*[7]

God made Adam *a priest* of the entire creation. He alone of all the creatures was capable of praising God. The entire universe was entrusted to Adam so that Adam would bring to God a sacrifice of praise on their behalf.

- ### A short comment about *'the fall'*

This is not the topic of our discussion, but I just want to mention a brief point in this respect.

Adam was deceived by the serpent because of *'pride'* and the desire to be *a god* in separation from

---

7 Bishop Hilarion Alfeyev, The Mystery of Faith, p.66

God. In His original plan, God has actually created man for deification; yet, this deification can only be achieved through communion with God; it can never be achieved in separation from God.

This desire for deification in separation from God was the exact same sin of Lucifer which we read about in Isaiah 14: 12 – 14:

'How you are fallen from heaven, O Lucifer, son of the morning! How you are cut down to the ground, you who weakened the nations! For you have said in your heart: 'I will ascend into heaven, I will exalt my throne above the stars of God; I will also sit on the mount of the congregation on the farthest sides of the north; I will ascend above the heights of the clouds, I will be like the Most High.'

Both the angel and man desired to be like God; and so they fell. Thus, the *'I'* or the *'ego'* became the main motive which drives the conduct of the fallen man.

As a result, all values collapsed. One's own *'I'* occupied the first place while the second place was occupied by the object of one's lust. No place remained for God; God was forgotten.

This fall had catastrophic results on all creatures

and on everything in the world; everything was distorted; and man's nature totally changed as death entered it.

Yet, in His love, God has accomplished a great salvation for man that also includes the whole creation:

'For the earnest expectation of the creation eagerly waits for the revealing of the sons of God. For the creation was subjected to futility, not willingly, but because of Him who subjected it in hope; because the creation itself also will be delivered from the bondage of corruption into the glorious liberty of the children of God. For we know that the whole creation groans and labours with birth pangs together until now. Not only that, but we also who have the first-fruits of the Spirit, even we ourselves groan within ourselves, eagerly waiting for the adoption, the redemption of our body' (Romans 8: 19 – 23).

Chapter 2. Through His Word and Commandments

1. Our God is a God of Covenant

The word *'covenant'* refers to the act of God in freely establishing a mutually binding relationship with mankind.

Through the covenant, God bestows blessings on His people, conditionally and unconditionally. Conditionally, God blesses the person who obeys the terms of the covenant. Unconditionally, God bestows blessings on the person regardless of their obedience or disobedience to the terms of the covenant. This is because of His mercies.

God made a covenant with Noah, Abraham, Moses and David. God fulfilled these covenants and instituted and established the New Covenant in Christ which is for all people who trust in Him.

'Therefore he is the mediator of a new covenant, so that those who are called may receive the promised eternal inheritance, since a death has occurred that redeems them from the transgressions committed under the first covenant... And just as it is appointed for man to die once, and after that comes judgment, so Christ, having been offered once to bear the sins of many, will appear a second time, not to deal with sin but to save those who are eagerly waiting for him' (Hebrews 9: 15, 27, 28).

This topic of the covenant is so fundamental in knowing and experiencing God (see appendix 1 for a detailed biblical study about the *'covenant'*).

2. God gave His Word to mankind

In Deuteronomy 4: 45 we read about the testimonies, the statutes and the judgements of God:

'These are the testimonies, the statutes, and the judgments which Moses spoke to the children of Israel after they came out of Egypt' (Deuteronomy 4: 45).

In Deuteronomy 6: 1, we read about the commandments, the statutes, and the judgements:

'Now this is the commandment, and these are the statutes and judgments which the Lord your God has commanded to teach you, that you may observe them in the land which you are crossing over to possess' (Deuteronomy 6: 1).

In the New Testament, Jesus referred to the two great commandments: the love for God and the love for the neighbour:

'Then one of them, a lawyer, asked Him a question, testing Him, and saying, "Teacher, which is the great commandment in the law?" Jesus said to him, 'You shall love the Lord your God with all your heart, with all your soul, and with all your mind.' This is the first and great commandment. And the second is like it: 'You shall love your neighbour as yourself.' On these two commandments hang all the Law and the Prophets' (Matthew 22: 35 – 40).

God gave these commandments to man in order to help him and not to judge him. The commandments are like crutches that were given to man because the fall caused paralysis in man making him unable to walk with God or to be in fellowship with God. After the fall, it became easy for man to deviate and go astray because he became crippled. It also became possible for man to be deceived by the enemy or to seek fake freedom away from God (as in the case of the Prodigal Son, Luke 15). The darkness that came upon man's mind as a result of the fall made him think that the commandments are bondages; while they are essentially for the good of man, as written in Deuteronomy 10: 13: *'and to keep the commandments of the Lord and His statutes which I command you today **for your good'**.* The commandments also worked as our *tutor: 'Therefore the law was **our tutor** to bring us to Christ, that we might be justified by faith'* (Galatians 3:24).

God also gave us various testimonies that refer to Him and manifest Him:

o   In nature

'Because what may be known of God is manifest in them, for God has shown it to them. For since the creation of the world His invisible attributes are clearly seen, being understood by the things that are made, even His eternal power and Godhead, so that they are without excuse, because, although they knew God, they did not glorify Him as God, nor were thankful, but became futile in their thoughts, and their foolish hearts were darkened' (Romans 1: 19 – 21).

o In His saints

'When He comes, in that Day, to be glorified in His saints and to be admired among all those who believe, because our testimony among you was believed' (2 Thessalonians 1: 10).

Psalm 119 highlights the attributes of God and the help and strength that come to us from His word: whether His *commandments*, *statues* or *judgements*. The worshipping Psalmist reveals these matters to us through supreme prophetic inspiration and highlights how these matters can become living spiritual experiences in the various circumstances of life (See appendix 2 for a detailed study of Psalm 119).

Chapter 3. Through the Circumstances of Life

Everyone knows God through different circumstances in life including illnesses, trials and sufferings.

These circumstances help in leading each one on his path of perfection. God has a plan for each one. He leads each person in a special way through various circumstances to help him reach the common goal.

The Psalms in particular express and portray this kind of knowledge of God through circumstances and suffering. Also, Job wanted to understand why

God sent him all his sufferings. God displayed to him His wonders of nature so that Job might accept the mystery of His acts which surpass all understanding.

Such circumstances make the soul more sensitive to the presence of God. In fact, difficult circumstances which pierce our being, urge us towards _fervent prayer_.

Speaking about fervent prayer, St. Chrysostom says:

"Prayer stands in the first place; then comes, the word of instruction. And that is why the Apostles said: _'we will devote ourselves to prayer and to the ministry of the word'_ (Acts 6: 4). Paul does this when he prays at the beginning of his epistles so that, like the light of the lamp, the light of prayer may prepare the way for the word. If you accustom yourselves to pray fervently, you will not need instruction from your fellow servants because God Himself, with no intermediary, enlightens your mind."[8]

Difficulties arise because we often forget to see everything we have as gifts of God which we should share with others. God wants to make us distributers of His gifts so that our love towards others may increase.

---

8 Taken from: _'Incomprehensible Nature of God', St. John Chrysostom._

When our circumstances are favourable and things are well with us, and also when we are in difficult circumstances, we should think of the responsibility we have towards our brothers before God. This keeps the thought of God in our conscience all the time, in both the good and the difficult circumstances.

'For God speaks in one way, and in two, though man does not perceive it. In a dream, in a vision of the night, when deep sleep falls on men, while they slumber on their beds, then he opens the ears of men and terrifies them with warnings, that he may turn man aside from his deed and conceal pride from a man' (Job 33: 14 – 17).

'When the Son of Man comes in his glory, and all the angels with him, then he will sit on his glorious throne. Before him will be gathered all the nations, and he will separate people one from another as a shepherd separates the sheep from the goats. And he will place the sheep on his right, but the goats on the left. Then the King will say to those on his right, 'Come, you who are blessed by my Father, inherit the kingdom prepared for you from the foundation of the world. For I was hungry and you gave me food, I was thirsty and you gave me drink, I was a stranger and you welcomed me, I was naked and you clothed me, I was sick and you visited me, I was in prison and you came to me.' Then

the righteous will answer him, saying, 'Lord, when did we see you hungry and feed you, or thirsty and give you drink? And when did we see you a stranger and welcome you, or naked and clothe you? And when did we see you sick or in prison and visit you?' And the King will answer them, 'Truly, I say to you, as you did it to one of the least of these my brothers, you did it to me.' "Then he will say to those on his left, 'Depart from me, you cursed, into the eternal fire prepared for the devil and his angels. For I was hungry and you gave me no food, I was thirsty and you gave me no drink, I was a stranger and you did not welcome me, naked and you did not clothe me, sick and in prison and you did not visit me.' Then they also will answer, saying, 'Lord, when did we see you hungry or thirsty or a stranger or naked or sick or in prison, and did not minister to you?' Then he will answer them, saying, 'Truly, I say to you, as you did not do it to one of the least of these, you did not do it to me.' And these will go away into eternal punishment, but the righteous into eternal life' (Matthew 25: 31 – 46).

A prayer of a saint in this context:

'Oh my soul, help the one who suffers injustice; so you can escape from the hand of the one who wrongs you.'

To sum up:

All the circumstances and persons through whom God speaks to us are appeals from Him. They are living and transparent images of Him. He is the God who descends to us in multiple forms and situations, indeed in all situations and forms of our life.

Chapter 4. Through Some Qualities We Need to Acquire

These include:

1. Love: the first epistle of John

2. Keeping the commandments: from the writings of Apostle John

3. Having continual and unceasing spiritual hunger: the Samaritan woman, according to the understanding of the early Church

4. Purification and repentance

5. The stillness: being freed from the deceitful thoughts and delusions

6. Accepting sufferings with awareness and understanding their purpose (sometimes God tightens circumstances around us to show us that the divine love is seeking us and searching for us)

7. Faith: it is God's gift to man so that man can perceive the Person of God who is incomprehensible

1. Love and its connection to knowing God

- **1 John 4: 7 – 19**

'Beloved, let us love one another, for love is of God; and everyone who loves is born of God and knows God. He who does not love does not know God, for God is love. In this the love of God was manifested toward us, that God has sent His only begotten Son into the world, that we might live through Him. In this is love, not that we loved God, but that He loved us and sent His Son to be the propitiation for our sins. Beloved, if God so loved us, we also ought to love one another. No one has seen God at any time. If we love one another, God abides in us, and His love has been perfected in us. By this we know that we abide in Him, and He in us, because

He has given us of His Spirit. And we have seen and testify that the Father has sent the Son as Saviour of the world. Whoever confesses that Jesus is the Son of God, God abides in him, and he in God. And we have known and believed the love that God has for us. God is love, and he who abides in love abides in God, and God in him. Love has been perfected among us in this: that we may have boldness in the Day of Judgment; because as He is, so are we in this world. There is no fear in love; but perfect love casts out fear, because fear involves torment. But he who fears has not been made perfect in love. We love Him because He first loved us.'

In these inspired words of Apostle John, we see that man's communion with God is expressed through love.

Where there is no love, God is absent and there is no spiritual life!

Where love is, God is; and all righteousness!

The origin of man's love is in God and comes from God. God's love always comes first. People love God and love one another because God Himself has loved us first. God's love is shown and expressed in the creation and the salvation of the world.

All things were made *by*, *in*, and *for* Christ, the

Word of God and the *'Son of His love'* (Colossians 1: 13 – 17; John 1: 1 – 3; Hebrews 1: 2).

'He has delivered us from the power of darkness and conveyed us into **<u>the kingdom of the</u>** <u>Son of His love</u>*, in whom we have redemption through His blood, the forgiveness of sins. He is the image of the invisible God, the firstborn over all creation. For* **by Him** *all things were created that are in heaven and that are on earth, visible and invisible, whether thrones or dominions or principalities or powers. All things were created* **through Him** *and* **for Him***. And He is before all things, and* **in Him** *all things consist. And He is the head of the body, the church, who is the beginning, the firstborn from the dead, that in all things He may have the preeminence'* (Colossians 1: 13 – 17).

'In the beginning was the Word, and the Word was with God, and the Word was God. He was in the beginning with God. All things were made **through Him***, and without Him nothing was made that was made'* (John 1: 1 – 3).

'...has in these last days spoken to us by His Son, whom He has appointed heir of all things, **through whom** *also He made the worlds'* (Hebrews 1: 2).

When the world became sinful and dead, *'God so loved the world that He gave His only begotten Son, that whoever believes in Him should not perish but have everlasting life'* (John 3: 16); *'And if anyone hears My words and does not believe, I do not judge him; for I did not come to judge the world but to save the world'* (John 12: 47).

- We read more about love and the love of God in the following verses:

*'But God **demonstrates His own love** toward us, in that while we were still sinners, Christ **died for us'*** (Romans 5: 8).

*'But when **the kindness and the love of God** our Saviour toward man appeared, not by works of righteousness which we have done, but according to His mercy **He saved us**, through the washing of regeneration and renewing of the Holy Spirit, whom He poured out on us abundantly through Jesus Christ our Saviour, that having been justified by His grace we should become heirs according to the hope of eternal life'* (Titus 3: 4 – 7).

*'And now abide faith, hope, love, these three; but **the greatest of these is love'*** (1 Corinthians 13: 13). Love is the greatest virtue.

*'Love does no harm to a neighbour; therefore, **love is the fulfilment of the law'*** (Romans 13: 10). Love is the fulfilment of the Law.

*'But the **fruit of the Spirit is love,** joy, peace, long suffering, kindness, goodness, faithfulness'* (Galatians 5: 22). Love is the first and greatest fruit of the Spirit.

*'Now hope does not disappoint, because **the love of God has been poured out in our hearts** by the Holy Spirit who was given to us'* (Romans 5: 5).

- St. Simeon, the new theologian (10th/11th century) says:

O' Holy Love;

He who knows you not, has never tasted the sweetness of your mercies which only living experiences can give us.

But he who has known you, or have been known by you, can never have even the smallest doubt.

For You are the fulfilment of the Law;

You are the One who fills, burns, inflames, and embraces my heart with a measureless love.

You are the teacher of the prophets, the offspring of the apostles, the strength of the martyrs; the inspiration of the fathers and masters; and the perfection of all the saints.

Only you, O' Love, prepare even me
for the true service of God.[9]

2. Keeping the commandments

+ Jesus requests us to keep the commandments because they are eternal life.

*'For I have not spoken on My own authority; but the Father who sent Me gave Me a command, what I should say and what I should speak. And I know that **His command is everlasting life**. Therefore, whatever I speak, just as the Father has told Me, so I speak'* (John 12: 49, 50).

+ Jesus tells us that keeping the commandments would make Him reveal Himself and *manifest Himself* to us.

*'He who has My commandments and keeps them, it is he who loves Me. And he who loves Me will be loved by My Father, and I will love him and **manifest Myself to him'*** (John 14: 21).

+ Jesus says that keeping the commandments makes Him come with the Father and make their home in us.

'If anyone loves Me, he will keep My word; and My

---

9 St.Symeon, Hymns of love.

*Father will love him, and **We will come to him** and **make Our home with him'** (John 14: 23).*

+ Jesus draws our attention to the fact that He Himself, who is our example, has kept the commandments of His Father. He draws our attention to this so that we also may do as He did and keep the commandments. This in turn makes us abide in love.

*'If you keep My commandments, you will abide in My love, **just as I have kept My Father's commandments** and abide in His love'* (John 15: 10).

+ Apostle John associates *keeping the commandments* to the true *knowledge of God.* Anything which is different from this needs to be examined and is doubtful. He maintains that he who *'does not keep His commandments, is a liar'.* The Apostle also highlights that keeping the commandments **perfects us in the love of God.** As a result, we abide in Him and become steadfast in Him; we will know that we are in Him. We will then walk just as He walked; we will become in His likeness; we will become *'christs/messiahs'.*

*'Now **by this we know that we know Him, if we keep His commandments.** He who says, "I know Him," and does not keep His commandments, is a liar, and the truth is not in him. But **whoever keeps His word,** truly*

the **love of God is perfected in him.** *By this we know that we are in Him. He who says he abides in Him ought himself also to walk just as He walked'* (1 John 2: 3 – 6).

+ Keeping the commandments grants us to *abide in Him*; and He in us; it is a mutual abiding.

'Now he who keeps His commandments **abides in Him, and He in him**. *And by this we know that He abides in us, by the Spirit whom He has given us'* (1 John 3: 24).

+ Apostle John highlights that keeping the commandments is a sign of our love for God. He reminds us that this is not a burdensome matter because we are born of God and are granted to overcome the world; the world resists whoever keeps the commandments and, in Christ, we are granted victory over the world.

'By this we know that we love the children of God, when we love God and keep His commandments. For **this is the love of God, that we keep His commandments.** *And* **His commandments are not burdensome**. *For whatever is born of God overcomes the world. And this is the victory that has overcome the world—our faith. Who is he who overcomes the world, but he who believes that Jesus is the Son of God?'* (1 John 5: 2 – 5)

+ When one keeps the commandments, he is not only being obedient to God, but he also becomes united with Christ and acquires the mind of Christ; he becomes Christ-like.

+ Deification means that in every situation in life, we act and respond as Christ acted and responded; *'to walk just as He walked'* (1 John 2: 6).

+ The Sermon on the Mount provides us with all the divine standards we need so that we can continuously revise ourselves and our lives against them.

+ Let us also remember the words of Jesus about forgiving others:

'So My heavenly Father also will do to you if each of you, from his heart, does not forgive his brother his trespasses' (Matthew 18: 35).

'But if you do not forgive, neither will your Father in heaven forgive your trespasses' (Mark 11: 26).

+ Apostle Paul highlighted several points in his epistles which can help us in the practical aspect of keeping the commandments. Examples of these are found in Ephesians 4: 1 – 3; Ephesians 4: 25 – 32; Ephesians 5: 1 – 21; Ephesians 5: 22; 6: 9 (commandments for the family).

+ If we pay careful attention to the writings of the apostles we will notice that all the apostles gave great attention and importance to keeping the commandments.

3. Having continuous and unceasing spiritual hunger

This hunger comes as a result of the work of the Holy Spirit in the soul who never ceases to seek God.

As the soul perceives the holiness of God, it continually works on completing repentance in order to be purified from all the corruption and darkness that have entered the human nature by the fall. This purification is done through the work of the purifying and cleansing blood of Jesus—as one continues in the life of true repentance.

The Lord draws near to these souls gradually revealing to them supreme matters. This nearness of the Lord in itself increases the hunger. As a result, the inner spiritual stirring continues, progressively pushing the person forward towards God.

There is a wonderful paradox here. Drawing close to God reveals the need of the soul for more cleansing, purification and illumination; and hence it draws closer to God. At the same time, in the presence of God, the soul becomes more aware of her need for

Him; and hence her spiritual hunger increases. This reciprocal situation continues, creating increased hunger in the soul.

The early Church fathers referred to the Samaritan woman as an example of this hunger and thirst; they called her *'the truth-seeker'*. This understanding changed during the time of Reformation where the reformers preferred to present the Samaritan woman as an example of a sinner who repented, in order to encourage sinners to repent and receive the faith.

Yet, if we carefully read what is written about this woman, we will notice that her questions reveal great spiritual knowledge and constant hunger. This hunger was probably the cause of her several marriages, seeking someone who can fill and satisfy her hungry inner being.

We also see her great impact and influence on the people of her city when she evangelised them. If she was the kind of woman with a bad reputation, she would not have been able to evangelise her city and receive the attention of all who listened to her and responded to her call:

'The woman then left her water pot, went her way into the city, and said to the men, "Come, see a Man who told me all things that I ever did. Could this be the Christ?"

Then they went out of the city and came to Him' (John 4: 28 – 30).

We know from history that this woman became an evangelist with the apostles. The apostles gave her the Greek name *Photini* which means *'the enlightened one'*. They chose this name because they considered that she had received a light and a revelation from the Lord to the extent that she impacted the people of her city in a way that made them say: *'we know that this is indeed the Christ, the Saviour of the world'* (John 4: 42); even the disciples of Jesus were not able to say such a statement about Jesus!

We can thus conclude that:

This kind of spiritual hunger leads to receiving a divine light which continues to increase, revealing to the person the knowledge of salvation. It then lights the person's whole inner being.

We are in great need for this hunger which would fill us with the light of God and His presence in the soul, as the great Saviour!

Having spiritual hunger and thirst is one of the beatitudes which Jesus mentioned: *'blessed are those who hunger and thirst for righteousness, for they shall be filled'* (Matthew 5: 6).

It is quite noticeable that there is a feature in our generation which makes this hunger absent, even absent from the believers. This is actually due to certain matters which we do not pay attention to. When we fail to pay attention to such matters, we allow them to take away our spiritual hunger and thirst.

A person would have this hunger if he realises and senses his inner emptiness. We sometimes sense this, but we soon lose it. The reason behind this is that this generation, without noticing, have learned to fill their emptiness with matters that poison the spiritual appetite; and hence one loses the sense of hunger. This is similar to a person who contracts an illness which makes him lose his appetite for food.

Watching sexual things poisons the spiritual appetite because uncleanness poisons the spiritual appetite. Also, the many daily preoccupations and being busy, in addition to lack of prayer and lack of regular reading of the word of God poison the spiritual appetite.

To clarify, the deepest part in man's inner being is naturally and spontaneously directed towards God (because we were created in His image) and seeks to be united with Him. Yet, this part is no longer empty because it has been filled with other things and has become poisoned. As one goes through the stages of cleansing and illumination, as we explained earlier in the example of the Samaritan woman, *'the enlightened one'*, this deep part in man starts to proclaim this deep hunger. It thus draws God to come and dwell in it. It will then be filled with a *distinct divine presence*, accompanied with *divine authority*, bearing *special anointing* of the Holy Spirit which is so essential in serving and ministering this generation.

Let us; therefore, wake up, be careful, and be vigilant.

Let us lay aside the corrupting satisfactions.

The sexual madness which characterises our generation is a plan from the evil one to destroy the generation.

Let us stop resorting to other means of filling or satisfaction like: food, clothes, laziness, laxity, and seeking position or prestige.

All these matters have limited our spiritual hunger and limited the true infilling we receive.

We became satisfied with intellectual knowledge void of the spiritual experience.

The spiritual experience would drive us towards

more hunger and seeking after the unity
and communion with God.

4. Purification and repentance: the path of purification and freedom, being freed from lusts (passions and desires) and the ego

In the writings of Apostle Paul, we read the following words:

'And those who are Christ's have crucified the flesh with its passions and desires' (Galatians 5: 24).

'But put on the Lord Jesus Christ, and make no provision for the flesh, to fulfil its lusts' (Romans 13: 14).

From the writings of the Church fathers, we understand that there are three important things which we need to pay attention to; so that, these things would no longer hinder our spiritual life; our relationship with God; and our understanding of His will.

These three things are:

- The passions and desires (they need to be crucified)

- The natural instincts (they need to be controlled)

- The authority of the ego (we need to be freed from it)

These three things are the result of the fall and they hinder our life in Christ so much. Yet, we have been granted victory over them by the resurrection of Christ.

○ *Passions and desires (lusts)*

When the passions and lusts control a person, they make the flesh so dense and heavy; the soul is darkened; and the spiritual insight of the person becomes blinded.

Through the grace of redemption, we have been granted the ability to crucify them by exercising asceticism, which actually means *self-control*. Asceticism is not only meant for worshippers and monks, but it is also for all the believers.

In this context, Apostle Paul writes: *'So I always take pains to have a clear conscience toward both God and man'* (Acts 24: 16—ESV).

In its Greek origin, *'take pains'* refers to asceticism —according to its correct biblical understanding.

Asceticism opens the way for the work of the grace of God which is always so near to us and so sufficient: *'My grace is sufficient for you, for my power is made perfect in weakness'* (2 Corinthians 12: 9). The work of this sufficient grace which is so near can be hindered if we do not give it a chance; and that is if we refuse to accept the correct understanding of asceticism.

o   *Instincts*

This includes the instinct of eating and sexual instincts; they are all natural instincts that God has put in man for the continuity of his life on earth. These instincts are not wrong in themselves; but, if misused, they may become sins.

The fathers of the Church taught us that every instinct has 2 boundaries or limits; the first one is the signal for the good use of the instinct; and it enables the person to use the instinct according to the correct need. For example, the instinct of eating: its first movement signals the need for food so that the person may receive from it the energy he needs; while its last limit is being full. But, we sometimes spoil this instinct and turn it to be a cause for sin when we go beyond the limit; like eating without needing to; or continuing to eat after being full, just for pleasure. Also, we sometimes fail to exercise control on this instinct. This control can be exercised through times of fasting. When we fast we are sacrificing the natural need of the instinct; and hence it is controlled.

We read the same principle, regarding the sexual instinct, in the words of Apostle Paul addressing married couples, saying:

'The wife does not have authority over her own body, but the husband does. And likewise the husband does not have authority over his own body, but the wife does. Do not deprive one another except with consent for a time, that you may give yourselves to fasting and prayer; and come together again so that Satan does not tempt you because of your lack of self-control' (1 Corinthians 7: 4, 5).

'Let marriage be held in honour among all, and let the marriage bed be undefiled, for God will judge the sexually immoral and adulterous' (Hebrews 13: 4).

o   The ego

The ego dominates the person in various ways. When the ego is crucified by the power of redemption, the person would no longer sense neither pride nor humility; he becomes free from himself; free from the views of others regarding him; free from wrong thoughts about others and from negative images in his mind related to their conduct in certain situations in the past.

The freedom from lusts and passions; together with controlling the natural instincts and crucifying the ego, fill the soul with divine light and allows a steadfast and surpassing peace to enter the soul. Because of this, Apostle Paul writes saying: *'And the peace of God, which <u>surpasses all understanding</u>, will guard your hearts and your minds in Christ Jesus'* (Philippians 4: 7). Have you ever thought about this phrase: *'surpasses all understanding'*? It means that it is a peace that overflows filling the soul and covering the mind; keeping it in great peace and quietude.

5. The stillness: being freed from deceitful thoughts and delusions

The fall has afflicted the human mind with many negative changes which are so hindering to the spiritual life as well as the human life.

Fall did not only darken the mind of man, as man became cut off the source of Light when he was cut off his fellowship with God, but the mind also became filled with delusions, fantasies, and negative imaginations. It became easy for the mind to accept deceits, delusions, false unjustified fears, or day dreams. This is because the mind became exposed to the enemy; and so, it became easy for the enemy to throw in the mind many confused and mixed up things. Discernment is required to be able to separate those mixed up thoughts.

All these things hinder man's peace and hinder his spiritual walk.

The purpose of Christ's death and resurrection is to restore man to his original state before the fall.

This grace is available for us. But we need to learn to open our inner human being and also our minds, because there are many inner rooms in our soul which are closed and which are full of corruption and darkness that hinder us so much; even if we were unaware of that.

Isn't this what Ezekiel, the prophet, was referring to, in a prophetic language, when he spoke about the *'swamps and marshes'*? The swamps and marshes actually refer to the *'closed places'.*

'Then he said to me: "<u>This water flows toward the eastern region</u>, goes down into the valley, and enters the sea. When it reaches the sea, <u>its waters are healed</u>. <u>And it shall be that every living thing that moves, wherever the rivers go, will live</u>. There will be a very great multitude of fish, <u>because these waters go there; for they will be healed, and everything will</u>

live wherever the river goes. It shall be that fishermen will stand by it from En Gedi to En Eglaim; they will be places for spreading their nets. Their fish will be of the same kinds as the fish of the Great Sea, exceedingly many. But its <u>swamps and marshes will not be healed</u>; they will be given over to salt' (Ezekiel 47: 8 – 11).

As the closed rooms and areas in the land of our soul start to open up and get in touch with the grace of God, the work and light of resurrection penetrates our inner depth. As a result, the imaginations and deceitful thoughts would stop! All the thoughts of the mind and its divergences, the day dreams, the fears, the deceits, and the illusions would all be controlled. At this point, the soul starts to enter into the stage of stillness, the deep inner peace and quietude!

The fathers of the Church spoke about this and they called it the *stillness*; they understood the biblical references to this spiritual state and entered into this spiritual experience:

- *'<u>Be still</u>, and know that I am God'* (Psalm 46: 10).

When we silence and stop the usual activity of the mind and enter into *the stillness*, we will start to know God in a new way; we will receive a new knowledge of God.

- '*Be silent, all flesh, before the Lord, for He is aroused from His holy habitation*' (Zechariah 2: 13).

God wants to reveal Himself in special ways; and hence, change our circumstances and correct the direction of history as a whole. Yet, our disturbances and anxieties and the activity of the flesh and the mind hinder Him and tie up His Hands. Therefore, the prophet cries out saying: '*Awake, awake, put on strength, O arm of the Lord*' (Isaiah 51: 9). And also: '*Awake, awake! Put on your strength, O Zion*' (Isaiah 52: 1).

Saying: '*He is aroused*' also means that His arm is aroused and is awakened to start His great work. This great work will reveal Him; it will correct the disharmony of creation; and restore it from going astray from God's purposes. It will thus return, be realigned, and move towards its true and correct goal which is the coming of Christ and His reign.

By this, the bride of Christ would get more and more prepared as she gets rid of the hindrances around her; and hence, puts on her strength: '*Awake, awake! Put on your strength, O Zion*'.

Not only this, but also through *stillness*, the bride will have power and steadfastness, as prophet Isaiah says in another passage: *'in returning and rest you shall be saved; in quietness and confidence shall be your strength'* (Isaiah 30: 15).

6. Accepting sufferings; understanding their significance; and dealing with our sense of frustration, disappointment and despair

God did not promise us joy, but a cup!

He calls us to suffer for His sake because this will lead us to experience His glory:

'Beloved, do not think it strange concerning the fiery trial which is to try you, as though some strange thing happened to you; but rejoice to the extent that you partake of Christ's sufferings, that when His glory is revealed, you may also be glad with exceeding joy. If you are reproached for the name of Christ, blessed are you, for the Spirit of glory and of God rests upon you. On their part He is blasphemed, but on your part He is glorified' (1 Peter 4: 12 – 14)*.*

Christ went through suffering because He kept His Father's commandments (John 12: 49, 50); He came into conflict with the world. The same is expected to happen with anyone who is called by Christ to live the very same life of Christ.

- Hebrews 12: 4 – 11

'You have not yet resisted to bloodshed, striving against sin. And you have forgotten the exhortation which speaks to you as to sons: "My son, do not despise the chastening of the Lord, nor be discouraged when you are rebuked by Him; _for whom the Lord loves He chastens_, and scourges every son whom He receives." If you endure chastening, God deals with you as with sons; for what son is there whom a father does not chasten? But if you are without chastening, of which all have become partakers, then you are illegitimate and not sons. Furthermore, we have had human fathers who corrected us, and we paid them respect. Shall we not much more readily be in subjection to the Father of spirits and live? For they indeed for a few days chastened us as seemed best to them, but He for our profit, _that we may be partakers of His holiness_. Now no chastening seems to be joyful for the present, but painful; nevertheless, afterward it yields the peaceable fruit of righteousness to those who have been trained by it.'

This biblical passage helps us understand some important points about the significance of God's plan for us regarding suffering.

- o   The purpose of the suffering which God allows is the deep cleansing and purification from sin: *'You have not yet resisted to bloodshed, striving against sin.'*

o Yet, let us remember that He who allows this is our **Heavenly Father** and that He does this out of love (verses 6 & 7).

o The purpose of this is *'to be partakers of His holiness'* (verse 10). We should not forget the commandment which calls upon us saying: *'be holy, for I am holy'* (Leviticus 19: 2; 1Peter 1: 16; Leviticus 20: 26). It is the commandment of both testaments: the Old and the New.

o But, as the Apostle warns us, we only see and experience sorrow and pain during the suffering. However, with patience and perseverance and completing the time of suffering; these sufferings will finally bear and yield *'the peaceable fruit of righteousness'* (verse 11). The time of suffering is always under God's control and it never exceeds the limit that God has appointed in order to plough the land of our life and put in it new seeds (Isaiah 28: 24, 25).

Another important point in God's economy in allowing suffering is to deal with frustrations, disappointments and despair which are prominent features in our generation.

St. Silouan, a contemporary saint who reposed in 1938, suffered many severe and intense spiritual battles that aimed at quenching the roots of deep love and hunger in his soul. As he persevered and sought the Lord, Jesus appeared to him and taught him the following words, which later became a message for this generation to fight the disease of frustration, disappointment and despair (for those who receive it and understand it).

The message that Jesus gave him was:

'Keep your mind in hell and do not despair.'

'Hell', here, means the withdrawal of God's grace. This is a well-known experience to worshippers. A time comes when grace withdraws and it appears that God is so far or absent. This is called *'sacred forsakenness'*; it is a certain divine training which weans the soul from the visible and tangible, filling it with *divine light*. This divine light comes after this training is completed. The training goes on for a certain period. The grace of God determines the length of this period.

Yet, a living hope is granted as a grace which accompanies this training. It is a spiritual gift of hope in God which expels despair and hopelessness.

Later, when one sees the *'divine light'*, one is completely changed. For no one can see this light and stay the same as he was before!

7. Faith: the gift of God to man to be able to perceive the incomprehensible Person of God

The reason why God cannot be defined in a way that can help us know Him lies in His super-existentiality.

All the words which we can use to define something are of the order of existence and this order is definable.

But as for God, existence is not given to Him from outside; He Himself is the source of Existence. That is why God cannot be defined or named except through personal nouns, as He said to Moses: *'I am who I am'* (Exodus 3: 14).

There is no rational proof of God:

- o God alone is the criteria of His truth.

- o God alone is the argument for His Being.

- o God alone can never be a subject to logical demonstrations.

Therefore, faith is granted to all as **a gift** so that

God might bring His presence in every human soul!

God talks with us as Person to person.

Once the person receives this experience, every thing becomes a proof for the existence and activity of God.

The eyes of the person, who believes, open up and he sees God in all things.

At that time, *to believe* becomes something whichis totally *rational*; and *not to believe* becomes something which is *irrational*.

Part 3:

God's Ways in Revealing Himself in the Old Testament and in the New Testament

Chapter 1. God's Ways in Revealing Himself in the Old Testament

After discussing God's ways of revealing Himself to man, in a general way, we will now discuss in a specific way how God revealed Himself in the Old Testament; and then how He revealed Himself in the New Testament.

First: God's ways in revealing Himself in the Old Testament

In the Old Testament, God revealed Himself by using specific names that refer to Him. We notice that God did not reveal Himself using one specific name because He is God and not man. He is infinite and limitless and so we can never perceive Him or comprehend Him through one specific name.

The various names of God reveal, not only the Person of God, but also His ways in dealing with man. God saw man's need in a particular situation and He revealed to him the aspect of Himself related to the area of his need. As a result, the person sought God and was able to deal with the situation he was facing in an appropriate way. He dealt with it as God purposed and was not overcome by it; and hence did not open a door for the enemy to crush him or hinder God's purposes in his life.

In the Old Testament, the name was not only *the identification* of the person, but it was *the identity* as well. Often, a special meaning was attached to the name. Names had, among other purposes, an explanatory purpose. For example, the name *'Nabal'* which means *'fool'* was the target of Abigail's explanation to David: *'Please, let not my lord regard this scoundrel Nabal. <u>For as his name is, so is he; Nabal is his name, and folly is with him</u>! But I, your maidservant, did not see the young men of my lord whom you sent'* (1 Samuel 25: 25).

Throughout the books of the Old Testament, God reveals Himself to us through His names. Studying these names will help us to understand who God really is, in a deeper and better way. The meanings of God's names reveal the central Personality and nature of the One who bears them.

In the Lord's Prayer, we repeat the phrase *'hallowed be Your name'*. To hallow a thing is to make it holy or to set it apart to be exalted as being worthy of absolute devotion. To hallow the name of God is to regard Him with complete devotion and loving admiration. God's name is of the utmost importance and we should never take His name lightly (Exodus 20:7; Leviticus 22:32); but we should always rejoice in it and think deeply upon its meaning.

A study in the names of God as revealed in the Old Testament

1. EL SHADDAI (elshad-di): All-Sufficient One, Lord God Almighty

El Shaddai occurs **7** times in the Old Testament.

- **Meaning and Derivation:**

El is another name that is translated **'God'**. It can be used in conjunction with other words to designate various aspects of God's character.

Many scholars believe that **Shaddai** is derived from the Hebrew word **'shad'** which means **'breast'**.

Some other scholars believe that the name is derived from an Akkadian word **'Šadu'** which means **'mountain'**; suggesting *strength and power*.

This name refers to God who completely nourishes, satisfies, and supplies His people with all their needs, as a mother would her child.

'Shaddai' being connected with the word for God **El**, denotes a God who freely gives nourishment and blessing; He sustains.

- **This name first occurred in Genesis 17: 1**

'When Abram was ninety-nine years old, the Lord appeared to Abram and said to him, "I am Almighty God; walk before Me and be blameless' (NKJV).

'And when Avram was ninety and nine shanah, Hashem appeared to Avram, and said unto him, I am El Shaddai; walk before Me, and be blameless' (OJB).

We notice that God revealed Himself to Abram according to Abram's need at that time. As Abram advanced in age and the promise of having descendants was not yet fulfilled, Abram started to despair (Genesis 15: 2). At this point, God made a covenant with Abram (Genesis 17: 4, 9) and revealed Himself to Abram as God El Shaddai, the Almighty, the strong and irresistible.

God drew near Abram with motherly tenderness to embrace Abram in His love—because God knew and understood Abram's pain and fears. As mentioned earlier, *Shaddai* also means the breast of a mother and refers to motherliness.

In similar situations, like those which Abram had gone through, we need to remind ourselves that God wants to draw near to us with His motherliness, tenderness, and the cover of His glory (His Shekhinah) to destroy our fear, doubt, and perplexity.

Examples of other references where *El Shaddai* occurred:

o **Genesis 28: 3**

'May <u>God Almighty</u> bless you, and make you fruitful and multiply you, that you may be an assembly of peoples' (NKJV).

'And <u>El Shaddai</u> bless thee, and make thee fruitful, and multiply thee, that thou mayest be a kahal amim' (OJB).

Jacob was leaving his parents' house and the place where he grew up and he was going to sojourn away from his home. Through the prayer and blessing of his father, Isaac, God was being presented to Jacob as the God Almighty, *El Shaddai*, who will be for Jacob like a mother who embraces, destroys the fear and strengthens in weakness.

- ○ **Genesis 35: 11**

'Also God said to him: <u>I am God Almighty</u>. Be fruitful and multiply; a nation and a company of nations shall proceed from you, and kings shall come from your body' (NKJV).

'And Elohim said unto him, <u>I am El Shaddai</u>; be fruitful and multiply; a Goy (nation) and a Kehal Goyim shall be from thee, and Melechim shall come out of thy loins' (OJB).

Jacob has just returned from the east to restart his life in Bethel. What awaits him? How will he start? There must have been many questions inside Jacob. Therefore, God presents Himself to Jacob as the Almighty, El Shaddai, who embraces, assures, secures, and strengthens through His irresistible power.

- ○ **Genesis 48: 3**

'Then Jacob said to Joseph: "<u>God Almighty appeared to me</u> at Luz in the land of Canaan and blessed me' (NKJV).

'And Ya'akov said unto Yosef, <u>El Shaddai appeared unto me</u> at Luz in Eretz Kena'an, and made on me a brocha' (OJB).

Jacob was approaching the end of his life on earth and he was telling his son, Joseph, about his life-experience with God. For Jacob, God was the Almighty God who had accompanied him like a tender loving mother who satisfies every need, strengthens and supports every day, throughout the whole path.

2. EL ELYON (el el-yone): The Most High

El Elyon occurs **28** times in the Old Testament. It occurs **19** times in the Psalms.

- ### Meaning and Derivation:

El is another name that is translated *'God'*. It can be used in conjunction with other words to designate various aspects of God's character.

Elyon literally means *'Most High'* and is used both as an adjective or separately and independently throughout the Old Testament.

It expresses the extreme sovereignty and majesty of God and His highest pre-eminence.

When the two words are combined: *El Elyon*, it can be translated: *'the most exalted God'*.

- ### The name first occurred in Genesis 14: 18:

'Then Melchizedek king of Salem brought out bread and wine; he was the priest of <u>God Most High</u>' (NKJV).

'And Malki-Tzedek Melech Shalem brought forth lechem and yayin and he was the kohen of <u>El Elyon</u>' (OJB).

We notice that this name of God was first used in relation to the priest of God. The priest is someone who knows God as the Most High and he proclaims this Most High God during his priesthood ministry. Let us not forget that in the New Testament we are also priests, in the general spiritual sense.

In the following verse (19), we notice that this priest (Melchizedek) blesses Abram by God the Most High: *'blessed be Abram by God Most High'*. In other words, he was drawing the blessing from God the Most High to bring it to Abram. This is the true work of a priest. It is our work as well; we should bless others, even those who persecute us, for it is written: *'bless those who persecute you; bless and do not curse'* (Romans 12: 14).

In the following verse (20), Melchizedek blesses the Lord because He had strengthened Abram in his battle and Abram was able to defeat the enemy and restore Lot, his nephew: *'blessed be God Most High, who has delivered your enemies into your hand'*.

In Psalm 57: 2, we read how David cried out unto God because of Saul's chasing after him. In that instance, David called upon God, the Most High; the One who is above all circumstances: *'I will cry out to God Most High, to God who performs all things for me'*.

3. ADONAI (ad-o-noy): Lord, Master

Adonai occurs **434** times in the Old Testament. There is heavy usage of *Adonai* in Isaiah. It also occurs 200 times in Ezekiel alone and appears 11 times in Daniel Chapter 9.

- **Meaning and Derivation:**

Adonai is the verbal parallel to *Yahweh* and *Jehovah*.

***Adonai* is *plural*; the *singular* is *adon*.**

In reference to God, the plural *Adonai* is used.

When the singular *adon* is used, it usually refers to a *human lord*. *Adon* is used 215 times to refer to men. Occasionally in the Scripture and predominantly in the Psalms, the singular *adon* is used to refer to God as well.

To avoid violating the commandment *'Thou shalt not take the name of the Lord your God in vain'* (Exodus 20:7), *Adonai* is sometimes used as a substitute for *Yahweh*.

Adonai can be translated literally as, *'my lords'*, both plural and possessive.

- **There are 4 names of God that appear numerously in the Old Testament:**

    o   Adonai is one of these names and it appears 434 times.

The other 3 names which appear numerously are:

    o   Yahweh: Lord, Jehovah; this appears 6, 519 times.

    o   Elohim: God, Judge, Creator; this appears 2,000 times.

    o   Jehovah Sabaoth: Lord of Hosts; and this appears 280 times.

Each of these names has significance and a special purpose. We will explain the meaning of the other 3 names as we get to them in the course of this study.

- ***Adonai* is first used in Genesis 15:2:**

But Abram said, "Lord God, what will You give me, seeing I go childless, and the heir of my house is Eliezer of Damascus? (NKJV)

And Avram said, Adonai Hashem, what wilt Thou give me, since I go childless, and the Ben Meshek of my Bais is this Eliezer of Dameshek (Damascus)? (OJB)

Abram proclaimed the Lordship of God over all situations and circumstances. It is true that he sensed his barrenness and despair, yet, when God appeared to him and told him: *'Do not be afraid, Abram. I am your shield, your exceedingly great reward'* (Genesis 15:1), Abram sensed the Lordship of God as He spoke to him. And so, in the following verse, Abram brought his problem to the Lord proclaiming first and foremost God's Lordship saying: *'Lord God'*, *'Adonai Hashem'*.

We need to do as Abram did. We usually bring our problems before God; yet, in doing so, we often forget His Lordship. Let us proclaim the Lordship of God over the situations towards which we may have a sense of despair or feel crippled and unable to do anything to alter them.

4. YAHWEH (yah-weh): Lord, Jehovah

Yahweh occurs **6,519** times in the Old Testament. This name is used more than any other name of God.

• Meaning and Derivation:

Yahweh is the promised name of God. In Jewish tradition, this name of God is too holy to voice either aloud or to themselves or in silence.

It is actually spelled "YHWH" without vowels.

YHWH is referred to as the Tetragrammaton which simply means consisting of four letters.

YHWH comes from the Hebrew letters: Yud, Hay, Vav, and Hay.

While *YHWH* is first used in Genesis 2, God did not reveal Himself as *YHWH* until Exodus 3:14, 15.

The modern spelling as *'Yahweh'* includes vowels to assist in pronunciation. Many pronounce *YHWH* as *'Yahweh'* or *'Jehovah'*. We no longer know for certain the exact pronunciation.

During the third century A.D., the Jewish people stopped saying this name in fear of violating the commandment *'Thou shalt not take the name of the Lord your God in vain'* (Exodus 20:7). As a result,

Adonai is occasionally a substitute for *YHWH*.

- **Yahweh is first used in Genesis 2:4:**

'This is the history of the heavens and the earth when they were created, in the day that <u>the Lord God</u> made the earth and the heavens' (Genesis 2: 4, NKJV).

'These are the generations of heaven and earth when they were created, in the day that <u>Yahweh God</u> made earth and heaven' (Genesis 2: 4, LEB).

We notice that this name first occurred in relation to creation. God is the Creator; and so, He is in control of all things and dominates all things. God desired to make Himself known to Adam in this way to call Adam for fellowship with Him as the God who is the source of all creation. This is because Adam was called to be the prince, lord, and keeper of this creation—as we see in the second occurrence of the name in the following verse:

'Then <u>the Lord God</u> took the man and put him in the Garden of Eden <u>to tend and keep it</u>' (Genesis 2: 15, NKJV).

'And <u>Yahweh God</u> took the man and set him in the Garden of Eden to cultivate it and to keep it' (Genesis 2: 15, LEB).

5. JEHOVAH NISSI (yeh-ho-vaw'nis-see'): The Lord My Banner, The Lord My Miracle

Jehovah-Nissi occurs only **once** in the Old Testament, in Exodus 17:15.

· **Meaning and Derivation:**

Jehovah is translated *'the Existing One'* or *'Lord'*. The chief meaning of *Jehovah* is derived from the Hebrew word *Havah* meaning *'to be'* or *'to exist'*. It also suggests *'to become'* or specifically *'to become known'*. This denotes a God who unceasingly reveals Himself.

Nissi is derived from *Nes* (*nês*) which means *'banner'*. *Nes* is sometimes translated as *a pole* with an insignia attached. In battles, the opposing nations would fly their own flag on a pole at each of their respective front lines. This was to give their soldiers a feeling of hope and a focal point. God is for us a banner of encouragement to give us hope and a focal point.

· **This name first occurred in Exodus 17: 15:**

'And Moses built an altar and called its name, The-Lord-Is-My-Banner' (NKJV).

And Moshe built a Mizbe'ach, and called the shem of

it *Hashem Nissi* (*Hashem is my Standard [rallying point]*) (OJB).

This was the first battle which the people of Israel fought after their exodus out of the slavery in Egypt.

Here, the Lord is revealing to His army, His people, that He is the banner, the flag, which is lifted up above them; and that they fight and battle under this banner, under His protection, and for the sake of His purposes.

Moses also built an altar and called it: *The Lord-Is-My-Banner*. In Hebrew, it is a compound name where *'Nissi'* (Banner) is added to *'Lord'* and so it becomes: The Lord My Banner. The meaning here is that the Lord is our Banner inasmuch as we build up the altar of worship in our lives. This is a new meaning and a new dimension which we should add to our understanding about building prayer altars in our homes. As we build these altars, we should know that the Banner of the Lord is raised up on our homes and on our lives; therefore, He is the one who fights our battles for us!

In the Septuagint, the Greek translation of the Old Testament, the word Nissi (Banner) is translated καταφυγή (kataphyge) which means 'refuge'. Our altars of prayer are the place where we meet God as our refuge.

6. JEHOVAH-RAAH (yeh-ho-vaw'raw-aw'): The Lord My Shepherd

Jehovah-Raah (The Lord my Shepherd) is used in Psalm 23.

- **Meaning and Derivation:**

Raah is derived from *Rô'eh* which means **'shepherd'**. A shepherd is one who feeds or leads his flock to pasture:

'For thus says the Lord God: 'Indeed I Myself will search for My sheep and seek them out. As a shepherd seeks out his flock on the day he is among his scattered sheep, so will I seek out My sheep and deliver them from all the places where they were scattered on a cloudy and dark day' (Ezekiel 34: 11, 12).

An extended translation of this word, **'rea'**, is **'friend'** or **'companion'**. This indicates the intimacy God desires between Himself and His people.

When the two words are combined **Jehovah Raah**, it can be translated **'The Lord my Friend'**.

- **This name first occurred in Genesis 48: 15:**

'And he blessed Joseph and said, "The God before whom my fathers, Abraham and Isaac, walked, <u>the God who has been my shepherd</u> all my life long to this day' (ESV).

And he made on Yosef a brocha, and said, HaElohim, before whom my Avot Avraham and Yitzchak did walk, <u>HaElohim Who was Roeh to me</u> all my life long unto this day' (OJB).

The experience of the fathers about God is usually handed down to the children. Here, Jacob is handing down to his son, Joseph, this knowledge and experience of God as the Shepherd.

- **We read this also in the blessing of Jacob to his son, Joseph**:

'But his bow remained in strength, and the arms of his hands were made strong by the hands of the Mighty God of Jacob <u>from there is the Shepherd,</u> the Stone of Israel' (Genesis 49: 24 –NKJV).

'But his keshet (bow) remained steady, and the arms of his hands remain strong, from the hands of the Avir Ya'akov, from there, <u>from the Ro'eh,</u> Even Yisroel' (Genesis 49:24 –OJB).

Once again, through the blessing of his father, Joseph hears that God is the Shepherd, the Stone of Israel.

- **This knowledge and experience of God, the Shepherd, extended throughout all the generations**.

David heard it and he praised and chanted about it in his famous Psalm: 'The Lord is my Shepherd':

'*The Lord is my shepherd; I shall not want'* (Psalm 23: 1 –NKJV).

Hashem is my Ro'eh (Shepherd); I shall not lack' (Psalm 23: 1 –OJB).

Also in the songs of Asaph, we read:

'*Give ear, O Shepherd of Israel, You who lead Joseph like a flock; You who dwell between the cherubim, shine forth'* (Psalm 80:1 –NKJV).

'*Give ear, O Ro'eh Yisroel, Thou that leadest Yosef like a tzon; Thou that art enthroned between the Keruvim, shine forth'* (Psalm 80:1 –OJB).

7. JEHOVAH RAPHA (yeh-ho-vaw'raw-faw'): The Lord That Heals

Jehovah-Rapha (The Lord that Heals) is used in Exodus 15:26.

• Meaning and Derivation:

In Hebrew, the word **Rapha** (râpâ') means: **'to restore', 'to heal',** or **'to make healthful'.**

When the two words are combined together:

Jehovah Rapha, it can be translated: *'The Lord who heals'*.

Jehovah is the Great Physician who heals the physical and emotional needs of His people.

- ### The name first occurs in Exodus 15: 26:

'If you diligently heed the voice of the Lord your God and do what is right in His sight, give ear to His commandments and keep all His statutes, I will put none of the diseases on you which I have brought on the Egyptians. For <u>I am the Lord who heals you</u>' (NKJV).

'And said, If thou wilt diligently pay heed to the voice of Hashem Eloheicha, and will do that which is yashar in His sight, and will give ear to do His mitzvot, and be shomer over all His chok, I will put none of these machalah (diseases) upon thee, which I put upon the Egyptians; <u>for Ani Adonoi rofecha</u> (I am Hashem that healeth thee)' (OJB).

The people of God faced an important need in the wilderness and that was the need for water. There was only bitter water. For them, this meant illnesses and diseases; for if they use the bitter water, they will become ill.

Therefore, God revealed to His people a certain

Yet, God was reminding His people that He has not changed His purposes. He will visit the city; restore it; and dwell there. The Lord is There; Hashem Shammah!

Thus we can say: **Jehovah Shammah** is a symbolic name for the **earthly Jerusalem**. The name indicates that God has not abandoned Jerusalem, leaving it in ruins, but there will be restoration.

9. JEHOVAH TSIDKENU (yeh-ho-vaw' tsid-kay'-noo): The Lord Our Righteousness

Jehovah Tsidkenu occurs only two times.

- **Meaning and Derivation:**

Tsidkenu is derived from **Tsedek** (tseh'-dek) which means *'to be stiff straight,* or *righteous'*.

When the two words are combined: **Jehovah Tsidkenu**, it can be translated *'The Lord who is our Righteousness'*.

This name is mentioned only twice in the book of Jeremiah.

- **The name first occurred in Jeremiah 23: 6:**

'In His days Judah will be saved, and Israel will dwell safely; now this is His name by which He will be called:

THE LORD OUR RIGHTEOUSNESS' (NKJV).

'In his days Yehudah shall be saved, and Yisroel shall dwell safely; and this is Shmo whereby he shall be called _Adonoi Tzidkeinu'_ (OJB).

- **The name was then mentioned in Jeremiah 33: 16:**

'In those days Judah will be saved, and Jerusalem will dwell safely. And this is the name by which she will be called: _THE LORD OUR RIGHTEOUSNESS'_ (NKJV).

'In those days shall Yehudah be saved, and Yerushalayim shall dwell securely; and this is what she shall be called, _Hashem Tzidkeinu'_ (OJB).

- **We notice the following:**

The Lord our righteousness which is one of the names of God will also become the name of His people, Israel. It will also become the name of the city, Jerusalem, where God will dwell with His people.

This reminds us of the completion of the picture in the New Testament where we read the following words in the epistles:

'...Christ Jesus, who became for us wisdom from God— and righteousness and sanctification and redemption' (1 Corinthians 1: 30).

'...being justified freely by His grace through the redemption that is in Christ Jesus' (Romans 3: 24).

10. JEHOVAH MEKODDISHKEM (yeh-ho-vaw' M-qadash): The Lord Who Sanctifies You, The Lord Who Makes Holy

Jehovah Mekoddishkem occurs **two** times in the Old Testament.

- **Meaning and Derivation:**

Mekoddishkem is derived from the Hebrew word **qâdash** which means **'sanctify'**, **'holy'**, or **'dedicate'**.

Sanctification is the separation of an object or person to the dedication of the Holy.

When the two words are combined: **Jehovah Mekoddishkem**, it can be translated **'The Lord who sets you apart'**.

This name is mentioned twice in Exodus 31:13 and Leviticus 20:8.

- **The name first occurred in Exodus 31:13:**

'Speak also to the children of Israel, saying: 'Surely My Sabbaths you shall keep, for it is a sign between Me and

you throughout your generations, that you may know that *I am the Lord who sanctifies you'* (NKJV).

'Speak thou also unto the Bnei Yisroel, saying, Verily My Shabbatot ye shall be shomer over; for it is an ot (sign) between Me and you throughout your dorot; that ye may have da'as that I am Hashem Who doth set thee apart as kodesh' (OJB).

- **The name was then mentioned in Leviticus 20: 8:**

'And you shall keep My statutes, and perform them: I am the Lord who sanctifies you' (NKJV).

'And ye shall be shomer over My chukkot, and do them: I am Hashem who sets you apart as kodesh' (OJB).

- **We notice the following:**

After the people came out of slavery, God reminded them of their need for sanctification which they would receive through the Lord and through their obedience to Him.

He gave them the Sabbath as a sign of sanctification and setting apart.

He also gave them the commandments and the statutes which if they obey, they would be sanctified. This is because these commandments and statutes would be like a channel that connects them with God, the source of their holiness and sanctification.

11. EL OLAM (elo-lawm'): The Everlasting God, The God of Eternity, The God of the Universe, The God of Ancient Days

El Olam is first used in Genesis 21:33.

• Meaning and Derivation:

El is another name that is translated ***'God'*** and can be used in conjunction with other words to designate various aspects of God's character.

Olam is derived from the root word ***'lm*** which means ***'eternity'***. ***Olam*** literally means ***'forever'***, ***'eternity'***, or ***'everlasting'***.

When the two words are combined: ***El Olam***, it can be translated: ***'The Eternal God'***.

• The name first occurred in Genesis 21: 33:

'Then Abraham planted a tamarisk tree in Beersheba, and there called on the name of the Lord, the Everlasting God' (NKJV).

'And Avraham planted an eshel (tamarisk tree) in Beer-Sheva, and called there on the Shem of Hashem El Olam' (OJB).

God revealed to Abraham this special feature of Himself as the Everlasting God. If Abraham was unable to perceive these dimensions in the Person of God, God would not have revealed this matter to him.

At that time, Abraham had been sojourning as a stranger in the land of the Philistines for many days. He knew that he had not yet possessed the land which God had promised him; yet he planted this tamarisk tree with eyes directed upwards to the Eternal God. The sojourning made him settle and dwell in the Eternal God not in the land which was temporary and which would pass away one day.

- **The same name is mentioned in Isaiah 26: 4 and Jeremiah 10: 10:**

  o Isaiah 26: 4

'Trust in the Lord forever, for in YAH, the Lord, is everlasting strength' (NKJV).

'Trust ye in Hashem forever; for in G-d Hashem is Tzur Olamin' (OJB).

Isaiah, the prophet, is drawing the attention of the people to God the Everlasting, at a time of difficult circumstances and when everything around them was being shaken (Isaiah 24: 1).

○   Jeremiah 10: 10

'But the Lord is the true God; He is the living God and <u>the everlasting King</u>. At His wrath the earth will tremble, and the nations will not be able to endure His indignation' (NKJV).

'But Hashem is the Elohim Emes, He is the Elohim Chayyim, and the Melech <u>Olam</u>; at His wrath ha'aretz shall tremble, and the Goyim shall not be able to endure His indignation' (OJB).

Jeremiah, the prophet, is reminding the people of the Everlasting God at a time when they were surrounded by false idols by which they were deceived and to which they were attracted.

12. ELOHIM (el-o-heem'): God, Judge, Creator

Elohim occurs over **2,000** times in the Old Testament.

• **Meaning and Derivation:**

Elohim is translated ***'God'***.

The derivation of the name *Elohim* is debatable to most scholars. Some believe it is derived from ***'êl'*** which originates from the root ***'wl'*** which means ***'strong'***.

Others think that *Elohim* is derived from another two roots: **'lh'** which means **'god'** in conjunction with **'elôah** which means **'fear'**.

And still others presume that both **'êl** and **Elohim** come from **'eloah'**.

- **This name first occurred in Genesis 1: 1:**

'In the beginning <u>God</u> created the heavens and the earth' (NKJV).

'In the beginning <u>Elohim</u> created hashomayim (the heavens, Himel) and haaretz (the earth)' (OJB).

In Hebrew, this name is in the plural form. This reminds us that the first revelation about God at the very opening of the books of the Scriptures (Genesis 1: 1) is in the plural form because God is a Trinity. The work of God, the Creator, is a collaborative work of the Trinity. Yet, this required a long preparation of humanity to be able to perceive it, because the mind of humanity has been darkened by the fall. This collaborative work of the Trinity was revealed in the New Testament.

- **The name is then mentioned in many other references.**

It is used to show God, the Creator, the Judge, and

the God, in the sense that He is the only God of Israel; in contrast, to the nations around them who had multiple gods. He is the Only God who is in control of all matters that concern man; and He is the source of all the needs of man.

13. QANNA(kan-naw'): Jealous, Zealous

Qanna occurs **six** times in the Old Testament.

- **Meaning and Derivation:**

Qanna is translated *'jealous'*, *'zealous'*, or *'envy'*.

- **The name first occurred in Exodus 20: 5:**

'You shall not bow down to them nor serve them. <u>For I, the Lord your God, am a jealous God</u>, visiting the iniquity of the fathers upon the children to the third and fourth generations of those who hate Me' (NKJV).

'Thou shalt not tishtacheveh to them, nor serve them; <u>for I Hashem Eloheicha am an El kanna</u>, visiting the avon Avot upon the Banim unto the third and fourth generation of them that hate Me' (OJB).

This jealousy is not in the sense we usually understand this word. We understand it differently because of our fallen nature. But, it is actually a jealousy associated with the marital union between man and God. It reveals the great extent of the love that God has for man. God desires to unite with man in a special kind of unity which is in the likeness of the marital unity.

The reason for this unity is to protect man from the enemies that surround him; the enemies are essentially the devils who desire to destroy man, whether directly or indirectly through evil people or circumstances.

The other reason for this unity is that God would be the source of abundance, blessing, and comfort for man through His love. Through this unity, man will be able to find satisfaction for his needs and will be able to complete the divine purpose of his temporary existence on earth.

This name with the same meaning is used six more times in the books of the Old Testament.

Further references to the name Qanna: Exodus 34:14 Deuteronomy 4:24; Deuteronomy 5:9; Deuteronomy 6:15.

14. JEHOVAH JIREH (yeh-ho-vaw'yir-eh'): The Lord Will Provide

Jehovah-Jireh occurs only **once** in Genesis 22: 14.

- **Meaning and Derivation:**

Jehovah-Jireh is a symbolic name given to Mount Moriah by Abraham to preserve the memory of the intervention of God in the sacrifice of Isaac by providing a substitute for the imminent sacrifice of his son.

- **This name was mentioned only once in Genesis 22: 14:**

'And Abraham called the name of the place, <u>The-Lord-Will-Provide</u>; as it is said to this day, "In the Mount of the Lord it shall be provided' (NKJV).

'And Avraham called the name of that place <u>Hashem Yireh</u>: as it is said to this day, "In the mount of Hashem it shall be provided' (OJB).

Abraham received this revelation about God on the day he offered his son, Isaac; and so, he called the mountain: *The Lord Will Provide.* This same mountain, Mount Moriah, is the mountain on which the temple was later built (2 Chronicles 3: 1).

Abraham experienced something miraculous which he did not expect. Isaac, his son, whom he had offered out of obedience to the Lord, was restored to him; and the Lord sent Abraham a ram to offer instead of Isaac.

This is a reference to Christ, who in the fullness of time was to offer Himself as a sacrifice for our salvation.

At the same time, it is a constant reminder for man that he possesses nothing, even what comes out of one's own body: his children. Everything is a gift from God who provides. He is the One who grants the children and provides man's material needs in this present age; so that man may gradually realise his need for the greatest gift, God's gift of salvation for man. This was through sending His Son to be incarnated to save us through the sacrifice of Himself.

If God gives and grants to this extent, will there be anything which man needs and asks for that God will not provide! It is written: *'Ask and it will be given to you; seek, and you will find; knock and it will be opened to you'* (Matthew 7: 7).

Therefore, Apostle Paul writes:

'He who did not spare His own Son, but delivered Him

up for us all, how shall He not with Him also freely give us all things?' (Romans 8: 32)

This name constantly reminds us that God is near and desires to grant us all that we need. Let us; therefore, come to Him and ask of Him; for it is written:

'The Lord is near. Be anxious for nothing, but in everything by prayer and supplication with thanksgiving let your requests be made known to God' (Philippians 4: 5b, 6 —LEB).

15. JEHOVAH SHALOM (yeh-ho-vaw'shaw-lome'): The Lord Is Peace

Jehovah-Shalom occurs only **once** in Judges 6: 24.

- **Meaning and Derivation:**

Shalom is a derivative of **shâlêm** which means to **'be complete'** or **'sound'**.

Shalom is translated **'peace'** or **'absence of strife'**.

Jehovah-Shalom is the name of an altar built by Gideon in Ophrah.

- **This name was mentioned only once in Judges 6: 24:**

'So Gideon built an altar there to the Lord, and called it <u>The-Lord-Is-Peace</u>. To this day it is still in Ophrah of the Abiezrites' (NKJV).

'Then Gid'on built a Mizbe'ach there unto Hashem,

and called it <u>Hashem Shalom</u>; unto this day it is yet in Ophrah of the Aviezri' (OJB).

God appeared to Gideon at a time when Gideon was in pain and agony because of the state of Israel who were intensely besieged by the enemies, the Midianites, to the extent that they were greatly impoverished and lacking daily sustenance (Judges 6: 1 – 6).

Gideon was groaning for the salvation of Israel; yet, he felt crippled and had many questions and was perplexed (Judges 6: 11 – 14). His questions revealed that his heart was so preoccupied by God's matters and God's people. He had a different heart from everyone else.

Therefore, God appeared to him to fill him with peace and sent him forth strengthened with divine power to save Israel from the Midianites.

16. JEHOVAH SABAOTH (yeh-ho-vaw' se ba'ôt): The Lord of Hosts, The Lord of Powers

Jehovah and *Elohim* occur with *Sabaoth* over **285** times. It is most frequently used in Jeremiah and Isaiah.

- **Meaning and Derivation:**

Sabaoth (s^e bâ'ôt) means *'armies'* or *'hosts'*.

Jehovah Sabaoth can be translated *'The Lord of Armies'*. This name denotes His sovereignty over every army, both spiritual and earthly. The Lord of Hosts is the king of all heaven and earth (Psalm 24:9-10; Psalm 84:3; Isaiah 6:5).

- ***Jehovah Sabaoth* is first used in 1 Samuel 1:3:**

'This man went up from his city yearly to worship and sacrifice to <u>the Lord of hosts</u> in Shiloh. Also the two sons of Eli, Hophni and Phinehas, the priests of the Lord, were there' (NKJV).

'And this man went up out of his city yearly to worship and to sacrifice unto <u>Hashem Tzva'os</u> in Shiloh. And the two banim of Eli, Chophni and Pinchas, the kohanim of Hashem, were there' (OJB).

This name refers to God as the Lord of hosts/armies; whether the visible ones: the army of Israel who went through many battles to enter the land of promise and after entering as well; or, the invisible ones: the enemies (the devils); and also the heavenly hosts (the angels) and the firmament (the sun, moon, sea); all are under His control and all surrender to the Lord of hosts and perform His will.

In this context, we remember, for example, that the sun had to stand still until Joshua completed the battle (Joshua 10: 12, 13). Also, at the time of the crucifixion of Christ, the sun had set for three hours and there was darkness over all the land (Matthew 27: 45). And when Jonah was fleeing Tarshish from the presence of the Lord, the sea raged (Jonah 1: 4). All these are *'the hosts'* or *'sabaoth'*, in Hebrew. The word *'hosts'* refers to all these creations (the sun, the sea, etc.). God is the Lord of these creations: the Lord of hosts; He is their Creator and the one who directs them to serve His purposes all the time.

- **Further references of the name *Jehovah Sabaoth* in the Old Testament:**

1 Samuel 1:11; 1 Samuel 17:45; 2 Samuel 6:18; 2 Samuel 7:27; 1 Kings 19:14; 2 Kings 3:14; 1 Chronicles 11:9; Psalm24:10; Psalm 48:8; Psalm 80:4; Psalm 80:19; Psalm 84:3; Isaiah 1:24; Isaiah 3:15; Isaiah 5:16; Isaiah 6:5; Isaiah 9:19; Isaiah 10:26; Isaiah 14:22; Jeremiah 9:15; Jeremiah 48:1; Hosea 12:5; Amos 3:13; Micah 4:4; Nahum 3:5; Haggai 2:6; Malachi 1:6.

Closely connected to the topic of the names of God is the topic of the attributes of God.

Attributes of God

When we speak of God's attributes, we are talking about those characteristics that help us to understand who God truly is.

We will highlight some of these attributes, putting them into two main categories: *Divine attributes* and *Spiritual attributes*.

I.   Divine Attributes

1. Infinity

God knows no boundaries. He is without measure. God is not subject to any of the limitations of humanity or His creation.

o   Genesis 21: 33

'*Then Abraham planted a tamarisk tree in Beersheba, and there called on the name of <u>the LORD, the Everlasting God</u>.*'

o   Deuteronomy 33: 27

'<u>*The eternal God*</u> *is your refuge and underneath are <u>the everlasting arms;</u> He will thrust out the enemy from before you, and will say, 'Destroy!'*"

- Isaiah 40: 28

'Have you not known? Have you not heard? The everlasting God, the LORD, the Creator of the ends of the earth, neither faints nor is weary. His understanding is unsearchable.'

- Psalm 90: 2

'Before the mountains were brought forth, or ever You had formed the earth and the world, even from everlasting to everlasting, You are God.'

2. Sovereignty

Sovereignty means that God is in control of everything that happens.

Yet, man still has a free will and is responsible for his choices in life.

God's sovereignty is a huge source of comfort to the believer because it helps him to know that no matter how chaotic any situation may seem, he should not fear because God is in charge and is on the throne.

God is the Supreme Being who answers to no one and who has the absolute right to do with His creation as He desires.

- ○ Genesis 14: 19

'Blessed be Abram of <u>God Most High</u>, possessor of heaven and earth; and blessed be <u>God Most High</u>, who has delivered your enemies into your hand.'

- ○ Exodus 18: 11

'Now I know that the Lord is <u>greater than all the gods</u>.'

- ○ Psalm 115: 3

'But our God is in heaven; he <u>does whatever he pleases</u>.'

- ○ Isaiah 46: 10

'Declaring the end from the beginning and from ancient times things that are not yet done saying, 'My counsel shall stand, and <u>I will do all My pleasure</u>.'

- ○ Matthew 10: 29

'Are not two sparrows sold for a copper coin? And not one of them falls to the ground <u>apart from your Father's will</u>.'

- ○ Romans 9: 15

'For He says to Moses, "I will have mercy <u>on whomever I will have mercy</u>, and I will have compassion on whomever I will have compassion.'

o   Ephesians 1: 11

'In Him also we have obtained an inheritance, being predestined according to the purpose of Him who works all things <u>according to the counsel of His will</u>.'

o   1 Timothy 6: 15

'...which He will manifest in His own time, He who is the blessed and only Potentate, <u>the King of kings and Lord of lords</u>.'

o   1 Peter 3:17

'For it is better, if it is <u>the will of God,</u> to suffer for doing good than for doing evil.'

3. Eternity

Eternity refers to God's timeless nature. God has no beginning and no end.

- ***God is perfect in that He surpasses all time and temporal limitations***

o   Exodus 3: 14

And God said to Moses, "I AM WHO I AM."

o   Hebrews 13: 8

'Jesus Christ is the same yesterday, today, and forever.'

- **God is unlimited by time**

  o Psalm 90: 4

  'For a thousand years in Your sight, are like yesterday when it is past, and like a watch in the night.'

  o 2 Peter 3: 8

  'But, beloved, do not forget this one thing, that with the Lord one day is as a thousand years, and a thousand years as one day.'

- **God is the Creator of the ages (i.e., of time itself)**

  o Hebrews 1: 2

  '...has in these last days spoken to us by His Son, whom He has appointed heir of all things, through whom also <u>He made the worlds</u>.'

  o Hebrews 11: 3

  'By faith we understand that <u>the worlds were framed by the word of God</u>, so that the things which are seen were not made of things which are visible.'

- **He exists through endless ages**

  o Psalm 90: 2

  'Before the mountains were brought forth, or ever

You had formed the earth and the world, even _from everlasting to everlasting_, You are God.'

- o Psalm 93: 2

'Your throne is established _from of old_; You are _from everlasting_.'

- o Psalm 102: 12

'But You, O Lord, _shall endure forever_, and the remembrance of Your name to all generations.'

- o Ephesians 3: 21

'To Him be glory in the church by Christ Jesus _to all generations, forever and ever_. Amen.'

4. Omnipresence

God is perfect in that He transcends all space and spatial limitations, being present everywhere. This allows Him to interact in any place at any times, even in multiple places simultaneously. Being present in all locations, there is no place we can go and not be in His presence.

- ▪ **_The universe cannot contain God_**

  - o 1 Kings 8:27

'But will God indeed dwell on the earth? Behold, heaven

and the heaven of heavens cannot contain You.'

- ○ Job 11: 7 – 9

'Can you search out deep things of God? Can you find out the limits of the Almighty? They are higher than heaven—what can you do? Deeper than Sheol—what can you know? Their measure is longer than the earth and broader than the sea.'

- ○ Isaiah 66: 1

'Thus says the LORD: heaven is My throne, and earth is My footstool. Where is the house that you will build Me? And where is the place of My rest?'

- ○ Acts 7: 48, 49

'However, the Most High does not dwell in temples made with hands, as the prophet says: 'heaven is My throne, and earth is My footstool. What house will you build for Me? Says the LORD, or what is the place of My rest?'

- ▪ **God is present everywhere**

- ○ Psalm 90: 1, 2

'LORD, You have been our dwelling place in all generations. Before the mountains were brought forth, or ever You had formed the earth and the world, even from everlasting to everlasting, You are God.'

- Psalm 139: 7 – 10

'Where can I go from Your Spirit? Or where can I flee from your Spirit? If I ascend into heaven, You are there; If I make my bed in hell, behold, you are there. If I take the wings of the morning, and dwell in the utter most parts of the sea, even there your hand shall lead me, and Your right hand shall hold me.'

- Matthew 18: 20

'For where two or three are gathered together in My name, I am there in the midst of them.'

- Matthew 28: 20

'...teaching them to observe all things that I have commanded you; and lo, I am with you always, even to the end of the age.'

- Acts 17: 28

'...for in Him we live and move and have our being, as also some of your own poets have said, 'for we are also His offspring.'

- **God fills all things**
  - Jeremiah 23: 23, 24

"Am I a God near at hand?" says the LORD, "And not a God afar off? Can anyone hide himself in secret places, so I shall not see him?" says the LORD; "Do I not fill

- ○ Ephesians 1: 23

'which is His body, the fullness of Him who _fills all in all._'

- ○ Ephesians 4:10

'He who descended is also the One who ascended far above all the heavens, that He might _fill all things._'

- ○ Colossians 3: 11

'...where there is neither Greek nor Jew, circumcised nor uncircumcised, barbarian, Scythian, slave nor free, but _Christ is all and in all._'

5. Omnipotence

God has the unlimited power to accomplish anything He wants.

- **_Nothing is too hard_**
  - ○ Genesis 18: 14

'_Is anything too hard for the LORD?_ At the appointed time I will return to you, according to the time of life, and Sarah shall have a son.'

- ○ Jeremiah 32: 17

'Ah, Lord GOD! Behold, You have made the heavens and

the earth by Your great power and outstretched arm. *There is nothing too hard for you.'*

    o   Jeremiah 32: 27

'Behold, I am the LORD, the God of all flesh. Is there anything too hard for Me?'

    o   Zechariah 8: 6

Thus says Yahweh of hosts: 'Even if it seems impossible to the remnant of this people in those days, should it also seem impossible to me?' declares Yahweh of hosts' (LEB).

    o   Matthew 3: 9

'...and do not think to say to yourselves, 'we have Abraham as our father.' For I say to you that God is able to raise up children to Abraham from these stones.'

- **All things are possible**

    o   Job 42: 2

'I know that You can do everything, and that no purpose of Yours can be withheld from You.'

    o   Psalm 115: 3

'But our God is in heaven; He does what He pleases.'

- o   Matthew 19: 26

'With God all things are possible.'

- o   Mark 10: 27

But Jesus looked at them and said, "with men it is impossible, but not with God; for <u>with God all things are possible</u>."

- o   Mark 14: 36

And He said, "Abba, Father, <u>all things are possible for You</u>. Take this cup away from me; nevertheless, not what I will, but what You will."

- o   Luke 1:37

'For with God nothing will be impossible.'

- o   Luke 18: 27

But He said, "The things which are impossible with men <u>are possible with God."</u>

- o   Romans 11:36

'For of Him and through Him and to Him are all things, to whom be glory forever. Amen.'

- o   Ephesians 1: 11

'In Him also we have obtained an inheritance, being predestined according to the purpose of Him who

works all things according to the counsel of His will.'

- ○ Hebrews 1: 3

'He (God's Son) upholds all things by the word of His power.'

6. Omniscience

God possesses **perfect knowledge** and therefore has no need to learn.

Omniscience means all-knowing. God knows everything, and **His knowledge is infinite**. It is impossible to hide anything from God.

- ▪ ***Perfect in knowledge***

- ○ Job 37: 16

'Do you know how the clouds are balanced, those wondrous works of Him who is <u>perfect in knowledge</u>?'

- ○ Psalm 147: 5

'His (God's) <u>understanding is infinite</u>.'

- ○ Acts 15: 18

'<u>Known to God</u> from all eternity are all His works.'

- ○ Romans 11: 33

'Oh the depth of His riches both of the wisdom

and knowledge of God! How unsearchable are His judgments and His ways past finding out!'

- o Hebrews 4:13

'And there is no creature hidden from His sight, but all things are naked and open to the eyes of Him to whom we must give account.'

- ▪ *Knows the heart*

- o 1 Samuel 16: 7

But the LORD said to Samuel, "Do not look at his appearance or at his physical stature, because I have refused him. For the LORD does not see as man sees; for man looks at the outward appearance, but <u>the LORD looks at the heart</u>."

- o 1 Chronicles 28: 9

'As for you, my son Solomon, know the God of your father, and serve Him with a loyal heart and with a willing mind; for <u>the LORD searches all hearts</u> and <u>understands all the intent of the thoughts</u>. If you seek Him, He will be found by you; but if you forsake Him, He will cast you off forever.'

- o 1 Chronicles 28: 17

"All this," said David, "the LORD made me understand in writing, by His hand <u>upon me,</u> all the works of these plans."

- Psalm 139: 1 – 4

'O LORD, You have <u>searched me and known me</u>. You know my sitting down and my rising up; You understand my thought afar off. You comprehend my path and my lying down, and are acquainted with all my ways. For there is not a word on my tongue, but behold, O LORD, You know it altogether.'

- Jeremiah 17: 10

'I, the LORD, <u>search the heart</u>, I test the mind, even to give every man according to his ways, according to the fruit of his doings.'

- Ezekiel 11: 5

Then the Spirit of the LORD fell upon me, and said to me, "Speak! Thus says the Lord: "Thus you have said, O house of Israel; for <u>I know the things that come into your mind</u>."

- 1 John 3: 20

'For if our heart condemns us, God is greater than our heart, and <u>knows all things</u>.'

- Romans 2: 16

'God will judge <u>the secret things of men</u> by Jesus Christ, according to my (Paul) gospel.'

- **Knows all events to come**

  o Isaiah 41: 22, 23

'Let them bring forth and show us what will happen; let them show the former things, what they were, that we may consider them, and know the latter end of them; or declare to us things to come. Show the things that are to come hereafter, that we may know that you are gods; yes, do good or do evil.'

  o Isaiah 42: 9

'Behold, the former things have come to pass, and new things I declare; before they spring forth I tell you of them.'

  o Isaiah 44: 7

'And who can proclaim as I do? Then let him declare it and set it in order for Me, since I appointed the ancient people. And the things that are coming and shall come, let them show these to them.'

7. Self-Existence

By self-existence, we refer to that unique attribute of God by which He has existed eternally and will always exist.

Unlike all other things that relate to our existence, God does not owe His being to any other thing. We owe our existence to our mother and father. And our earth owes its existence to God who created the world.

All events have causes. All creatures have been created, except for God. God is the uncaused cause and the uncreated Creator.

God did not depend upon anything outside Himself for His existence, nor will He ever depend upon anyone for it.

- o   Exodus 3:14

And God said to Moses, "I AM WHO I AM."

- o   Psalm 90: 2

'Before the mountains were brought forth, or ever You had formed the earth and the world, even from everlasting to everlasting, You are God.'

- o   John 1: 1 – 5

In the beginning was the Word, and the Word was with God, and the Word was God. He was in the beginning with God. All things were made through Him, and without Him nothing was made that was made. In Him was life, and the life was the light of men.

o   John 5: 26

'For as the Father has life in Himself, so He has granted the Son to have life in Himself.'

o   Colossians 1:15 – 17

'He is the image of the invisible God, the firstborn over all creation. For by Him all things were created that are in heaven and that are on earth, visible and invisible, whether thrones or dominions or principalities or powers. All things were created through Him and for Him. And He is before all things, and in Him all things consist.'

8. Immutability

God never changes. God does not change His mind. He does not change His plan, His covenants, His prophecies, or His justice. Our future is secure and eternal in Him.

o   Malachi 3: 6

'For I am the Lord, <u>I do not change</u>.'

o   James 1: 17

'Every good gift and every perfect gift is from above, and comes down from the Father of lights <u>with whom there is no variation</u> or shadow of turning.'

- ***God is consistent throughout all time***

  - Hebrews 13: 8

'Jesus Christ *is the same* yesterday, today, and forever.'

- ***God is good–all the time***

  - James 1: 17

'Every good gift and every perfect gift is from above, and comes down from the Father of lights, with whom there is no variation or shadow of turning.'

- ***He does not lie and is true to His word***

  - Numbers 23: 19

'God is not a man, that He should lie, nor a son of man, that He should repent. Has He said, and will He not do? Or has He spoken, and will He not make it good?'

- ***His love is never-ending***

  - Lamentations 3: 22, 23

'Through the LORD's mercies we are not consumed, because His compassions fail not. They are new every morning; great is Your faithfulness.'

- ***Though the universe will change, God never will***

○ Psalm 102: 25 – 27

'Of old You laid the foundation of the earth, and the heavens are the work of Your hands. They will perish, <u>but You will endure</u>; yes, they will all grow old like a garment; like a cloak You will change them, and they will be changed. <u>But You are the same,</u> and Your years will have no end.'

○ Hebrews 1: 10 – 12

And: "You, Lord, in the beginning laid the foundation of the earth, and the heavens are the work of Your hands. <u>They will perish, but You remain</u>; and they will all grow old like a garment; like a cloak You will fold them up, and they will be changed.<u> But You are the same,</u> and Your years will not fail.

II.   Spiritual Attributes

A. Holiness

This is the attribute that sets God apart from all created beings. It refers to His majesty and His perfect moral purity. There is absolutely no sin or evil thought in God at all.

His holiness is the definition of that which is pure and righteous in the entire universe.

Wherever God has appeared, such as to Moses at the burning bush, that place becomes holy, just for God having been there.

- o Exodus 3: 5, 6

Then He said, "Do not draw near this place. Take your sandals off your feet, for the place where you stand is holy ground." Moreover He said, "I am the God of your father-the God of Abraham the God of Isaac, and the God of Jacob." And Moses hid his face, for he was afraid to look upon God.

- o 1 Samuel 2: 2

'No one is holy like the Lord.'

- o Psalm 99: 2, 3

'The Lord is great in Zion, and He is high above all the peoples. Let them praise Your great and awesome name-He is holy.'

- o Isaiah 6: 3

'Holy, holy, holy is the Lord of hosts; the whole earth is full of His glory!'

- o Revelation 4: 8

'Holy, holy, holy, Lord God Almighty, who was and is and is to come!'

B. Righteousness

Righteousness is similar to holiness, but the difference is that holiness is internal; it is the state of the heart; while, righteousness is external; it refers to the conduct.

- ○ Genesis 18: 25

'Far be it from You to do such a thing as this, to slay the righteous with the wicked, so that the righteous should be as the wicked; far be it from You! <u>Shall not the Judge of all the earth do right</u>?'

- ○ Psalm 19: 7 – 9

'The law of the Lord is perfect, converting the soul; the testimony of the Lord is sure, making wise the simple; the statutes of the Lord are right, rejoicing the heart; the commandment of the Lord is pure, enlightening the eyes; the fear of the Lord is clean, enduring forever; <u>the judgments of the Lord are true and righteous</u> altogether.'

- ○ Psalm 145: 17

'<u>The Lord is righteous</u> in all His ways, gracious in all His works.'

- ○ Jeremiah 9: 24

"But let him who glories glory in this, that he understands and knows Me, that I am the Lord,

exercising lovingkindness, judgment, and righteousness in the earth. For in these I delight," says the Lord.

C. Justice

God is the ultimate judge over the lives and actions of men.

There seems to be so much injustice in the world: men lie, cheat, steal, and kill all the time with no seeming repercussions. True justice is not found in this earthly realm, but in the true realm (the eternal heavenly realm).

In God's justice, we can find comfort for all the wrongs done against us and against mankind.

- o Genesis 18: 25

'Far be it from You to do such a thing as this, to slay the righteous with the wicked, so that the righteous should be as the wicked; far be it from You! Shall not the Judge of all the earth do right?'

- o Exodus 34: 6, 7

'The Lord, the Lord God, merciful and gracious, longsuffering, and abounding in goodness and truth, keeping mercy for thousands, forgiving iniquity and transgression and sin, by no means clearing the guilty,

visiting the iniquity of the fathers upon the children and the children's children to the third and the fourth generation.'

   o   Nehemiah 9: 32, 33

'However You are just in all that has befallen us.'

   o   Romans 9:14 – 33

'What shall we say then? Is there unrighteousness with God?'

   o   Psalm 99: 4

'The King's strength also <u>loves justice</u>; You have established equity; You have executed justice and righteousness in Jacob.'

   o   Romans 1: 32

'Who, knowing <u>the righteous judgment of God</u>, that those who practice such things are deserving of death, not only do the same but also approve of those who practice them.'

   o   1 Peter 1: 17

'And if you call on the Father, who <u>without partiality judges</u> according to each one's work, conduct yourselves throughout the time of your stay here in fear.'

D. Mercy

God has demonstrated this attribute in abundance with respect to mankind. Nearly from the beginning of our existence, we have deserved nothing but wrath. Having sinned and fallen short of eternal life in glory, we can do nothing to commend ourselves to or defend ourselves before God. But thankfully, God has been so amazing in His mercy.

o   Psalm 6: 4

'Return, O Lord, deliver! Oh, save me <u>for Your mercies' sake</u>!'

o   Hebrews 4: 16

'Let us therefore come boldly to the throne of grace, <u>that we may obtain mercy</u> and find grace to help in time of need.'

o   Romans 9: 23, 24

'And that he might make known the riches of His glory on the vessels of mercy, which He had prepared beforehand for glory, even us whom He called, not of the Jews only, but also of the Gentiles?'

o   Ephesians 2: 4

'God, who is <u>rich in mercy</u>...'

- Titus 3: 5

'Not by works of righteousness which we have done, but <u>according to His mercy</u> He saved us, through the washing of regeneration and renewing of the Holy Spirit.'

- 1 Peter 1: 3

'Blessed be the God and Father of our Lord Jesus Christ, who <u>according to His abundant mercy</u> has begotten us again to a loving hope through the resurrection of Jesus Christ from the dead.'

E. Love

We all have a basic understanding of what love is, but we are unable to comprehend the depths of true love. This is the love of God. God is the genesis of love; He is its source.

- Deuteronomy 7: 7, 8

'The Lord did not set His love on you nor choose you because you were more in number than any other people, for you were the least of all peoples; but <u>because the Lord loves you</u>, and because He would keep the oath which He swore to your fathers, the Lord has brought you out with a mighty hand, and redeemed you from the house of bondage, from the hand of Pharaoh king of Egypt.'

- John 14: 31

'But that the world may know that I love the Father, and as the Father gave Me commandment, so I do.'

- Romans 5: 5, 8

'Now hope does not disappoint, because <u>the love of God has been poured out</u> in our hearts by the Holy Spirit who was given to us... But God <u>demonstrates His own love</u> toward us, in that while we were still sinners, Christ died for us.'

- Romans 8:35, 39

'Who shall separate us from the love of God? Shall tribulation, or distress, or persecution, or famine, or nakedness, or peril, or sword...nor height nor depth, nor any other created thing, shall be able to separate us from the love of God which is in Christ Jesus our Lord.'

- 1 John 4: 8, 16

'He who does not love does not know God, for God is love.... And we have known and believed the love that God has for us. God is love, and he who abides in love abides in God, and God in him.'

F. Goodness

One of the most intrinsic attributes of God is His

goodness. He is the source of goodness; He alone is the measure of what we truly know to be good. To the Christian, the goodness of the Lord is his rest, assurance and security.

- o Exodus 34: 6, 7

'The Lord, the Lord God, merciful and gracious, longsuffering, and abounding in goodness and truth, keeping mercy for thousands, forgiving iniquity and transgression and sin, by no means clearing the guilty, visiting the iniquity of the fathers upon the children and the children's children to the third and the fourth generation.'

- o Psalm 25: 8

'Good and upright is the Lord.'

- o James 1:17

'Every good gift and every perfect gift is from above, and comes down from the Father of lights with whom there is no variation or shadow of turning.'

- o Romans 8: 28

'And we know that all things work together for good to those who love God, to those who are the called according to His purpose.'

G. Wisdom

God has all wisdom. He works everything out for the good of his people, and for the display of his glory. Even when things look the worst, God is carrying out his perfect wisdom. He is the Father who truly knows best. He never fails, never lacks any foresight, and never makes mistakes. He knows all, and plans all.

o   1 Kings 3: 28

'And all Israel heard of the judgment which the king had rendered; and they feared the king, for they saw that the wisdom of God was in him to administer justice.'

o   1 Kings 4: 29

'And God gave Solomon wisdom and exceedingly great understanding, and largeness of heart like the sand on the seashore.'

o   Romans 11: 33

'Oh, how great are God's riches and wisdom and knowledge! How impossible it is for us to understand His decisions and His ways!'

o   James 1: 5

'If any of you lacks wisdom, let him ask of God, who gives to all liberally and without reproach, and it will be given to him.'

H. Faithfulness

Everything that God has promised will come to pass. His faithfulness guarantees this fact. He does not lie. What He has said in the Bible about Himself is true. Jesus said that He is the Truth. This is important for us because it is on His faithfulness that our hope of eternal life rests. We can trust Him to always keep His promises.

- ■ *God is faithful to the faithful*

    - ○ Deuteronomy 7: 7 – 9

'The Lord did not set His love on you nor choose you because you were more in number than any other people, for you were the least of all peoples; but because the Lord loves you, and because He would keep the oath which He swore to your fathers, the Lord has brought you out with a mighty hand, and redeemed you from the house of bondage, from the hand of Pharaoh king of Egypt. Therefore know that the Lord your God, He is God, <u>the faithful God</u> who keeps covenant and mercy for a thousand generations <u>with those who love Him and keep His commandments</u>.'

- ■ *God is faithful through calamity*

    - ○ Lamentations 3: 22, 23

'Through the LORD's mercies we are not consumed,

because His compassions fail not. They are new every morning; great is Your faithfulness.'

- **God is faithful to fulfill His promises**

  o 1 Thessalonians 5: 24

  'He who calls you is faithful, who also will do it.'

  o Hebrews 10: 23

  'Let us hold fast the confession of our hope without wavering, for <u>He who promised is faithful</u>.'

- **His faithfulness is immeasurable and endures forever**

  o Psalm 36: 5

  'Your mercy, O LORD, is in the heavens; Your faithfulness reaches to the clouds.'

  o Psalm 119: 90

  'Your faithfulness endures to all generations; You established the earth, and it abides.'

Chapter 2. God's Ways in Revealing Himself in the New Testament

In this context, we read the following very clear words:

'God, who at various times and in various ways spoke in time past to the fathers by the prophets, has in these last days spoken to us by His Son, whom He has appointed heir of all things, through whom also He made the worlds; who being the brightness of His glory and the express image of His person, and upholding all things by the word of His power, when He had by Himself purged our sins, sat down at the right hand of the Majesty on high' (Hebrews 1: 1 – 3).

This leads us to a study about the Person of the Son and His work; but before this we need to discuss how God reveals Himself as the Trinity.

Part 4

The Holy Trinity

Chapter 1. The Mystery of the Holy Trinity

Love always assumes that there are two *"I's"* who love each other.

But, as human beings, our love always has the print of being *unperfected*. This unperfected love between us assumes the existence of perfect love between the divine Persons (of the Trinity) with a common being. Our love finds its meaning and essence in the fact that we are created in the image of the Holy Trinity—the origin and source of our love.

Only a God who is Father and Son explains the

whole reality of earthly paternity and son-ship. These relations receive a spiritual quality from God through the Holy Spirit. All the fatherhood and all the son-ship are gifts bestowed on us by that divine and supreme source of Fatherhood and Son-ship.

Our continuance and perfection as persons is assured to eternity through the Trinity.

The doctrine of the Trinity constitutes the foundation, the infinite reservoir, the power, and the model of our growing eternal communion. Yet, it also urges and motivates us to continuously grow and think in the spirit; and helps us to go beyond any level we may have reached in our personal communion with God and among ourselves.

The Trinity and Salvation

The Trinity reveals itself essentially in the work of salvation and that is why the Trinity is the basis on which salvation stands.

Because a Triune God exits, one of the divine Persons (the Son) was incarnated. Through this incarnation, the Son placed all His human brothers within this relationship, as sons to the heavenly Father; or, indeed, placed His Father within a paternal relationship to all men.

Through the incarnate Son, we enter into filial communion with the Father; while *through the Holy Spirit*, we pray to the Father or speak with Him as sons.

Through grace, the Holy Spirit identifies Himself with us so that, through grace, we may identify ourselves with Him.

Through grace, the Holy Spirit eliminates the distance between our 'I' (person) and His 'I' (person); creating, between us and the Father, the same relation that He has with the Father and the Son.

In the incarnate Son, we become sons by grace; and in the Spirit, we gain the consciousness and boldness which come from being sons.

The Holy Spirit makes humanity fit to participate in the love which the Son has towards the Father (John 17: 26 –*that the love with which You loved Me may be in them, and I in them*).

The purpose of the revelation of the Trinity is to draw us, through grace, into the *filial relationship* which the Son has with the Father.

Christ, the Son, is equal in being with the Father and stands in filial relation to the Father. At the same time, **He is the Man** who prays and sacrifices Himself to the Father for the sake of His human brothers, teaching them that they, in turn, should pray and sacrifice themselves.

Unity is Inspired and Strengthened by the Holy Trinity:

The most suitable image for the Holy Trinity is found in human unity of being and personal distinction.

We need to promote greater unity among ourselves as distinct human persons. In order to achieve this, we must be helped by the very grace of the Holy Trinity, the very power of the Trinity which strengthens unity within us without weakening us as persons.

The Relation of the Persons of the Trinity

According to the fathers of the Church, this relation can be likened to the three surpassingly bright and transparent suns. They are reciprocally comprised in one another and appear in one another, bearing one complete infinite light which is undivided.

The Father is the sun in the sense of the **paternal existence and essence** of infinite light, causing the Son to appear in Him.

The Son is the sun in the sense of a **reflection** of the whole of that infinite light which exists and dwells in the Father.

The Father projects Himself as a filial sun and views Himself through His Son. He reveals Himself more luminously through His Son.

The Father also projects Himself as another sun, as the Holy Spirit, revealing Himself more luminously as paternal sun and revealing the Son in the same way, as filial sun.

The same infinite light exists and dwells in the three Persons of the Trinity; they are like three modes (reflections). Each Person of the Trinity appears shining through the other two, bearing the same infinite light and being in them, and they being in Him.

Perichoresis

This term was suggested by St. John of Damascus (7th / 8th century). It then became a well-known term in the Patristic theology of the Holy Trinity.

The word 'perichoresis' comes from two Greek words, *peri*, which means "around," and *chorein*, which means "to give way" or "to make room." It can be translated "rotation". It refers to the mutual intersecting of the three Persons of the Godhead. It expresses intimacy and reciprocity among the

Persons of the Godhead.

It is the fellowship of three co-equal Beings perfectly embraced in love and harmony and expressing an intimacy that no one can humanly comprehend. There is nothing that separates the Persons of the Trinity or interrupts the mysterious interchange of perichoresis.

It can be imagined as a diagram showing three circles intersecting in the centre with each circle intersecting the others perfectly and multidimensionally, as they rotate about a common centre of divine love.

Perichoresis allows the individuality of the persons to be maintained, while insisting that each person shares in the life of the other two.

Perichoresis refers to the continuous relationship among the Persons of the Trinity.

To sum up, a subject's joy of existence is in the communion with other subjects. In the perfect unity of the Trinity, the awareness of the other two subjects and the subjects themselves who bear that awareness must be perfectly comprised and transparent in the awareness of each subject. This will be further clarified in the following point about *'divine intersubjectivity'.*

Divine Intersubjectivity and its Fruits

The spiritual character of the transparency of the divine persons can be expressed by the term *'intersubjectivity'*.

Intersubjectivity is the principle of one person's awareness of another person's awareness of a given thing. The principle of intersubjectivity applies to the Persons of the Trinity in an absolutely perfect manner.

What the Father sees as the Son, is essentially the Son's awareness of the Father. Because of the divine simplicity, the Son and the Son's awareness of the Father are identical. The Father sees his own being reflected in the Son. Conversely, when the Son sees the Father, He essentially sees the Father's awareness of the Son, because likewise the Father and the Father's awareness of the Son are identical. In the Father's awareness of the Son and the Son's awareness of the Father, we have the full and perfect operation of intersubjectivity. The intersubjectivity is so perfect and complete that the awareness of the Father and the Son form a single act of consciousness.

The Persons of the Trinity do not see anything as *object* in one another. Each Person experiences the others as pure subjects and experiences Himself as pure subject too. If there were anything in them which had the character of *object*, this would diminish their full openness to the other two subjects.

Full communion takes place only between persons who make themselves transparent as pure subjects. The more they are subjects, the more the relation between them is characterised by a greater degree of communication.

Each Person does not reveal his own 'I', but two Persons together reveal the other. Also, each pair of Persons does not reveal their own 'I's' but they place the other 'I' in the forefront, making themselves transparent for that one or hiding themselves beneath him. Therefore, in each Person of the Trinity, the other two are also visible.

St. Basil says: *"The Father reveals the Son...other times, the Son reveals the Father. Thus, the entire Godhead is revealed to you sometimes in the Father; and at other times in the Son and in the Holy Spirit."*[10]

Perfect love is manifested in this self-forgetting of each person for the other. This alone makes this unity, which is the opposite of individualism, possible.

The sin of individualism hinders us from

---

10 Dumitru Staniloae, Experiencing God, p.264

understanding the fullness of love and unity which is characteristic of the Holy Trinity. It is a unity which opposes individualism; yet, at the same time, it preserves the personal identity.

The unity of our nature had been dissolved away by sin. This can be re-established only through this mystery of the Trinity. Christ, who dwells in us, substitutes the 'I' of the Spirit for His own 'I' and vice versa. This, in turn, persuades us to substitute the 'I' of the Spirit and of Christ and of our neighbour for our own 'I'; hence, re-establishing the unity of our nature.

We can achieve our unification in God and among ourselves only through the work of the Holy Trinity. This is necessary in order to work out our salvation.

St. Maximous, the Confessor, 6th/7th century, maintains: *"Because of love, everyone attracts willingly his neighbour to him and prefers him as much as he rejected him before and wanted to be ahead of him."*[11]

The Trinity: Why three Persons?

The communion between two subjects (persons) can bring about a sense of joy and meaning to life. But this is not sufficient.

---

[11] Ibid. p.265

Communion between two is in itself a limitation because this kind of communion does not open up the entire horizon of existence. This is because while the two open themselves to one another, they close themselves off. The 'other' becomes both a window and a wall. Two cannot live only from their resources. They must be aware of a horizon which extends beyond them—though it is linked with both of them.

Only the third subject—one who can be partner in the communion—takes the two out of their uninterrupted loneliness. It is only through the third that the love between the two can be generous and become capable of extending to subjects outside themselves.

This is the sense in which the name of the Holy Spirit is so closely associated with love. Only through the Holy Spirit does the divine love radiate outwards.

The Procession of the Holy Spirit from the Father

The teaching of the early Church[12] about the procession of the Holy Spirit from the Father towards the Son and His shining forth from the Son towards the Father implies that the Son and the Father are neither confused nor separated from each other.

---

12 Ecumenical Council, 2nd in Constantinople, 381

In this sense, the Holy Spirit allows *'communion'* to take place in a special manner:

'The grace of the Lord Jesus Christ, and the love of God, and the communion of the Holy Spirit be with you all' (2 Corinthians 13: 14).

'Therefore if there is any consolation in Christ, if any comfort of love, if any fellowship of the Spirit, if any affection and mercy...' (Philippians 2: 1)

The Spirit saves us from a deadly loneliness. Because of this, He is the Comforter.

The Spirit bears witness to our conscience before God (1 Corinthians 2: 10 – 12) and through the Spirit, as His gift, God dwells in us (1 Corinthians 12: 3 – 11).

'But God has revealed them to us through His Spirit. For the Spirit searches all things, yes, the deep things of God. For what man knows the things of a man except the spirit of the man which is in him? Even so no one knows the things of God except the Spirit of God. Now we have received, not the spirit of the world, but the Spirit who is from God, that we might know the things that have been freely given to us by God' (1 Corinthians 2: 10 – 12).

'Therefore I make known to you that no one speaking by the Spirit of God calls Jesus accursed, and no one can

say that Jesus is Lord except by the Holy Spirit. There are diversities of gifts, but the same Spirit. There are differences of ministries, but the same Lord. And there are diversities of activities, but it is the same God who works all in all. But the manifestation of the Spirit is given to each one for the profit of all: for to one is given the word of wisdom through the Spirit, to another the word of knowledge through the same Spirit, to another faith by the same Spirit, to another gifts of healings by the same Spirit, to another the working of miracles, to another prophecy, to another discerning of spirits, to another different kinds of tongues, to another the interpretation of tongues. But one and the same Spirit works all these things, distributing to each one individually as He wills' (1 Corinthians 12: 3 – 11).

St. Athanasius (4th century) declares: *"But we apart from the Spirit are strange and distant from God, and by participation of the Spirit we are knit to the Godhead; so that our being in the Father is not ours, but is the Spirit's which is in us and abides in us, while by the true confession we preserve it in us."*[13]

---

13 Ibid. p.277

Chapter 2. Hypostases: Its Meaning and Implication for Our Lives

The word *'hypostases'* is a theological term which is often used in connection to the Trinity. It is usually said that the Trinity is three hypostases, that *'hypostasis'* means *'person'* and that God is three Persons in One special and distinct unit: the Father, the Son, and the Holy Spirit.

This explanation is true and correct; yet, it is incomplete. It reflects an incomplete understanding of the hypostases of the Trinity; especially in terms of its connection to our life –because we are created on

God's image and likeness.

If God is essentially a hypostasis in His Person, each one of us should also be a hypostasis.

What does this mean?

Since *'hypostasis'* means *'person'*, then, this means that each one of us is a *'person'*.

What is new about that?!

The word 'hypostasis' does not only mean a mere person—the way we linguistically understand it; it means more than that. It actually means *'a person who has fellowship with other persons; this fellowship is on an equal level and also on the level of necessity or inevitability'*—in the sense that this person cannot live his own person without the others.

There is a difference between an *'individual'* and a *'person'*. An individual lives in his individualism, not relying on others. If he relies on others for any reason, he would only deal with them from the outside. For example, he can seek others regarding an external need, such as food, drink, medicine, or a need of a doctor or a hospital, and the like; but, he would not seek others regarding a need related to his own being.

A person, on the other hand, realises that his need

of 'the other' is a need related to his being; he was created to live in fellowship with the other, and this other completes his own person!

This applies even in the case of a hermit. When his life is sanctified and the work of redemption extends in him, restoring his original image as was created by God, he realises the meaning of being created on God's image and so restores his *'hypostasis'*, being a *'person'*—in the same sense that this word is used to refer to the Trinity. As a result, this hermit would be in fellowship with other human beings despite being away from them in the flesh, living in solitude to worship. He would still feel their needs and would pray for them because he is one with them. He becomes Cosmic. This happens through the work of the Holy Spirit in him.

Based on this, we can also understand God's greatest commandment, as Jesus puts it, in Matthew 22: 35 – 40:

'You shall love the Lord your God...You shall love your neighbour <u>*as yourself*</u>*'.*

Because I am a *'hypostasis'*, a *'person'*, my own existence is associated with the other.

Remember also the words of the Lord in Matthew

25: 31 – 46, especially verses 40 and 45:

'Assuredly, I say to you, inasmuch as you did it to one of the least of these My brethren, you did it to Me' (Matthew 25: 40).

'Assuredly, I say to you, inasmuch as you did not do it to one of the least of these, you did not do it to Me' (Matthew 25: 45).

The other is the Person of Christ Himself. This means that I see Christ in that person; I see the face of God in him (refer to Genesis 33: 10 *'inasmuch as I have seen your face as though I had seen the face of God'*).

After wrestling with God and seeing God face to face in the previous chapter, Jacob's personality, his hypostasis, changed. When Jacob saw Esau, there was no anger between them because Jacob was bearing in his person (his hypostasis) the touch of God whom he had seen: *'For I have seen God face to face'* (Genesis 32: 30). Not only this, but also when Jacob saw Esau, he did not see him as an enemy who was to be fought; he actually saw the face of God in Esau: *'I have seen your face as though I had seen the face of God'.*

It is quite remarkable that in Greek, the word *'person'* is *'prosopon'* which is also translated *'face'*, because a person is identified by his face, his countenance. However, if he is living merely as an 'individual', it would be as though he loses his main God-given features and becomes void of any specific features which outline and identify his personality; what will remain will only be the features of the outer flesh and Jesus has said: *'the flesh profits nothing'* (John 6: 63).

Incarnation and the Fellowship of the Trinity:

When Jesus was incarnated, His Hypostasis bore a human nature and a divine nature: the human nature which He took from us through the Virgin Mary and His divine nature.

Therefore, if one is restored to his original personality, his hypostasis, he is called to enter into the fellowship of the Trinity through the Person of the Son. This is because one's human nature which has become a person, a hypostasis, is called to unite with Christ through His human nature. Through this unity, one can enter into the fellowship of the Trinity through the Person of the Son: *'But he who is joined to the Lord is one spirit with Him'* (1Corinthians 6: 17). This in turn leads one to find true favour with God, enter into the rest in God and be secure in Him as one becomes *'a member of the household of God'* (Ephesians 2: 19). One, thus, becomes as though

can do nothing' (John 15: 5).

'...that they all may be one, as You, Father, are in Me, and I in You; that they also may be one in Us, that the world may believe that You sent Me. And the glory which You gave Me I have given them, that they may be one just as We are one: I in them, and You in Me; that they may be made perfect in one, and that the world may know that You have sent Me, and have loved them as You have loved Me... And I have declared to them Your name, and will declare it, that the love with which You loved Me may be in them, and I in them' (John 17: 21 – 23, 26).

Notice the words of the Apostle where he says: *'you have been filled in Him'*. In His divine hypostasis, Christ bore the fullness of deity, when He was incarnated. When we unite with Him and be in Him, this same fullness flows in us and fills us, so, we become *'filled in Him'*!

Notice also the Apostle's words: *'filled with all the fullness of God'* and also *'the stature of the fullness of Christ'*.

How can all this be possible without true understanding of the hypostases and entering into the fellowship of the Son through His hypostasis!

We are hypostasis, persons, because redemption has restored to us this lost hypostasis—to be a person. Consequently, Christ can fill our inner man with His presence and we can reach the stature of the fullness of Christ. This is actually because we do not enter into this fellowship as individuals, but as hypostases. In other words, we enter it with others, the members of the body of Christ who will then be a *'perfect man'* (Ephesians 4: 13).

When we were baptised in Him, we were implanted into the Son: *'For by one Spirit we were all baptised into one body'* (1 Corinthians 12: 13). According to the Greek origin, the word *'baptised'* means *'implanted'*. In other words, we became branches implanted in the vine. We also became His flesh and His bones: *'For we are members of His body, of His flesh and of His bones'* (Ephesians 5: 30).

Jesus prayed this very thing before His crucifixion, asking and interceding that we may be one in Him:

'...that they all may be one, as You, Father, are in Me, and I in You; that they also may be one in Us, that the world may believe that You sent Me. And the glory which You gave Me I have given them, that they may be one just as We are one: I in them, and You in Me; that they may be made perfect in one, and that the world may know that You have sent Me, and have loved them

as You have loved Me. "Father, I desire that they also whom You gave Me may be with Me where I am, that they may behold My glory which You have given Me; for You loved Me before the foundation of the world. O righteous Father! The world has not known You, but I have known You; and these have known that You sent Me. And I have declared to them Your name, and will declare it, that the love with which You loved Me may be in them, and I in them." (John 17: 21 – 26).

Jesus started this prayer by saying: *'And this is eternal life, that they may know You, the only true God, and Jesus Christ whom You have sent'* (John 17: 3). The true knowledge of God is through Jesus Christ. The phrase *'whom You have sent'* is a reference to His incarnation. Through this fellowship, we can truly taste and experience the stream of the life of God, His eternal life!

Since we are in Christ, we cannot remain constrained in the circle of oneself or those around us: our families, friends, or even our spiritual groups and churches. We should have an impact which extends to the whole world. Using the early fathers' language, we should enter into the fact that the redeemed person (who is a hypostasis in Christ, united with Christ in the fellowship of His human nature) is universal! Because this person is in Jesus Christ, he can extend across all the heaven and earth. According to the early fathers, this is called the *Universality of Man* or the *Cosmic Manhood*[14].

We should not neglect this matter nor be oblivious of our responsibility. As much as we reach peace and reconciliation within ourselves and with others, this will extend to those around us. In such a way, we can have an impact on the peace and the state of the world, for the sake of Christ who groans because of the fire of the evil one which is setting the world aflame.

In this context, Apostle James writes:

'Where do <u>wars and fights</u> come from among you? Do they not come from your desires for pleasure that war in your members?' (James 4: 1)

The early fathers emphasised that every real change which we desire to see in others should start in us, remembering that we can impact the whole world if we do not neglect the fact that we are universal and cosmic. When we complete our inner battles and struggles, we shall add to the peace which will extend to others; it is the peace of God. It is written: *'Blessed are the peacemakers, for they shall be called sons of God'* (Matthew 5: 9).

However, because we are lovers of ourselves and

---

14 St. Bessarion the Great of Egypt (4/5th century); St. Gregory of Nyssa (4th century); St. Siloan the Athonite (reposed 1938) lovers of earthly things (2 Timothy 3: 1 – 5), we war and fight; and hence lose our peace and hinder the peace of those around us.

'But know this, that in the last days perilous times will come: For men will be <u>lovers of themselves</u>, lovers of money, boasters, proud, blasphemers, disobedient to parents, unthankful, unholy, unloving, unforgiving, slanderers, without self-control, brutal, despisers of good, traitors, headstrong, haughty, lovers of pleasure rather than lovers of God, having a form of godliness but denying its power. And from such people turn away!' (2 Timothy 3: 1 – 5)

In this context, St. Maximous the Confessor, 7th century, writes:

'We have preferred profane and material things to the commandments of love. And because we have attached ourselves to them, we fight against men; whereas, we ought to prefer the love of all men to all visible things and even to our own body' (The Ascetic life, 7).

Also, John Cassian, 4th/5th century, writes:

'The goal of peaceful improvement cannot be reached through decisions of others which is forever beyond our control, but is found rather in our own attitude! To be free from wrath is not dependant on

the perfection of others, but stems from our own virtue,
which is acquired through our own tolerance, not other
people's patience' (Institute VIII, 17).

These matters are so precious in God's sight; they
have cost Him to pour out His love and sacrifice to
the point of death. If we do not pay enough attention
to these precious matters, the alternative would
be sad and lamentable. Man needs to be in a state
of constant change and transformation; he cannot
remain in one static state. This means that if we
are not transformed into the image of Christ and
become *'holy icons'* bearing the presence of God
(like the early Christians who were called *'bearers of
God's presence'*), the hidden corruption in our fallen
nature will increase; the evils of the world around us
will besiege us more and more; and the enemy will
then imprint in us his evil image. As a result, we will
become mere 'dummies' instead of being 'icons'!

Other Fruits and Blessings

This understanding of the hypostases adds to
our unity as a body of Christ. If we enter into this
fellowship as hypostases (redeemed persons), we
will realise the fact that there is *One head for one body*.

This will correct and heal many false and confused
notions which hinder us and hinder the unity of the

body and the preparation of the bride of Christ.

Perceiving the above truths, allows us to enter into the fullness of the foretaste and experience of the son-ship which has been granted to us in Christ— becoming the children of the heavenly Father. We will thus know that this son-ship is a divine gift which is unchangeable; it does not depend on anything in us. We will also realise that it is such a great privilege.

All these great matters are associated with the seal of the Spirit which has been granted to us as children of the heavenly Father.

'Now He who establishes us with you in Christ and has anointed us is God, who also has <u>sealed us</u> and given us the Spirit in our hearts as a guarantee' (2 Corinthians 1: 21, 22).

'In Him you also trusted, after you heard the word of truth, the gospel of your salvation; in whom also, having believed, <u>you were sealed with the Holy Spirit of promise</u>, who is the <u>guarantee of our inheritance</u> until the redemption of the purchased possession, to the praise of His glory' (Ephesians 1: 13, 14).

This seal makes us become His own, His property; and this is the guarantee of our eternal inheritance.

Finally, we need to maintain the balance between

what has been granted to us and what has become our responsibility:

- In Christ, we have been granted an infinite and inexhaustible well of riches.

- In Christ, it has become our responsibility to keep this well open, to vigil on lifting up any hindrance which can cut us off from this source or which can make us not be fully connected to it; so that, we do not wither (John 15: 2, 6), but rather become a source of life for others (John 4: 14).

'Every branch in Me that does not bear fruit He takes away; and every branch that bears fruit He prunes, that it may bear more fruit... If anyone does not abide in Me, he is cast out as a branch and is withered; and they gather them and throw them into the fire, and they are burned' (John 15: 2, 6).

'...but whoever drinks of the water that I shall give him will never thirst. But the water that I shall give him will become in him a fountain of water springing up into everlasting life' (John 4: 14).

Further Insights into the Hypostases[15]

A deep understanding of the meaning of the 'hypostasis' is essential because this would help a lot in understanding the process of the true and deep transformation into Christ-likeness.

God is One God, but is three Persons, three hypostases: the Father, the Son, and the Holy Spirit.

We were created on the image and likeness of God. So, we too have the 'hypostatic principle' inside us.

Hypostatic Principle in Man

The 'hypostatic principle' is an important term coined by Elder Sophrony (1896 – 1993). He viewed the 'hypostatic principle' as the innermost primary and ultimate principle which constitutes the ontological core of the divine Being. The hypostatic principle was given to man as a divinely conferred power.

However, to activate this hypostatic principle, man needs to empty himself completely of his egoism, become humble, and keep the dual commandment of love towards God and towards his neighbour.

The entire ascetic life aims toward this goal, which

---

15 Archimandrite Zacharias, *Christ, Our Way and Our Life*, p. 17-29.

is the perfect fulfilment of man as being created in the image and likeness of God.

The hypostatic principle simply means that when man has increased spiritually through ascetic labour to the point where he becomes Christ-like, he becomes a real person, a 'hypostasis'.

The hypostatic principle in man develops and is perfected by this struggle to be united with Christ and to restore the divine image which was corrupted and lost by the fall. By this union with Christ, the power of Christ's Resurrection is transmitted to man, and his heart radiates the light of the glory of the knowledge in the Person of Jesus Christ.

One Triune God with Three Hypostases

God is One Triune God but three Hypostases. In this undivided Holy Trinity, there are three distinct aspects[16] of Being:

- The Hypostasis (Person)

- The Essence (nature)

- The Energy (act of motion)

From this triadological doctrine, we can draw the following four facts:

---

16 'As explained by Elder Sophrony, *'aspects'* do not refer to different modes; it just refers to three ontological categories (categories of being) which are applicable to God.

a. The Hypostasis is *the bearer* of the Essence; and the Essence is the *ontological content* of the Hypostasis.

The Hypostasis and the Essence are one Unity.

Each Hypostasis bears in itself the fullness of the divine Being. Thus, each Person is equal to the Triune Unity.

b. Each Hypostasis has everything in common with the other two Hypostases, apart from the particularity (uniqueness) of His Personhood.

To clarify:

The unoriginated Father, who is unbegotten, begets the Son outside time, conferring upon Him the totality of His Being; and issues the Spirit who proceeds from Him.

The Son is begotten from the Father; and lives totally in the Father and the Spirit.

The Holy Spirit proceeds pre-eternally from the Father; and reposes in the Son.

These three Hypostases or Persons constitute a pure *Fact of Being* which God Himself has revealed to man.

c. The unity and distinction between the Essence and the Energy in God:

Divine Energy expresses divine Essence as **Life**.

Divine Energy is God Himself—as the Essence of God is God Himself.

But, the Essence (the divine nature) remains completely supreme, incomprehensible, and incommunicable:

'who alone has immortality, dwelling in unapproachable light, whom no man has seen or can see, to whom be honour and everlasting power' (1 Timothy 6: 16).

'But He said, "You cannot see My face; for no man shall see Me, and live' (Exodus 33: 20).

Yet, the Energy (the very Life of God) can unite with humans (created beings who are granted reason).

d. The union of the *uncreated Energy* with the *created human nature*:

The union with the divine Energy (1 Corinthians 6: 17) deifies human beings, but it does not transform them into uncreated beings.

'But he who is joined to the Lord is one spirit with Him' (1 Corinthians 6: 17).

Divine Life which is poured out on human beings bridges the wide gap between the uncreated God and the created man.

Despite this distinction between Hypostasis, Essence, and Energy, we do not at all mean that Divinity is composed of various elements.

God is a *'living God'* because He is Personal. What pre-eminently lives is the Person, the Hypostasis, who possesses Nature & Energy.

Divine Love

The central and primary content of this divine Life is Love.

Divine Love is selfless, it is 'Kenotic'. This is another theological term which refers to Christ's emptying Himself: *'but emptied himself by taking the form of a slave, by becoming in the likeness of people. And being found in appearance like a man...'* (Philippians 2: 7 —LEB).

This is a fundamental characteristic of the divine Life of the three Hypostases, in which each Hypostasis is totally open to the others. This mutual self-emptying love is an indication of the humility of the divine Persons. It shows that each One lives with love in the other two and receives the witness of Truth from them!

The Word: the Son of God

Of the three Hypostases of the Holy Trinity, the Person of the Lord Jesus is the nearest to us because of His incarnation.

His Person contains both *the invisible Divinity* and *the whole of humanity*.

Thus, Christ has revealed to the world the truth of the hypostatic principle.

Man was formed by Christ, the Word. Thus, man bears in himself the hypostatic principle.

Because man was created on the image and likeness of God, he has been given a natural inclination towards God and a potential to receive the fullness of God's energies.

As much as man participates in the fullness of the energies of his Maker, his ontological content develops. The magnificence of man and his godlike qualities are manifested as he participates in God's energies. God's energies are the very reality of the divine existence.

Before the fall, man was crowned with glory:

'What is man that You are mindful of him, and the son of man that You visit him? For You have made him a

little lower than the angels, and You have crowned him with glory and honour' (Psalm 8: 4, 5).

'You have made him a little lower than the angels; You have crowned him with glory and honour, and set him over the works of Your hands' (Hebrews 2: 7).

If the fall had not happened, man would have continued in an incorruptible state and would have moved from one level of glory to the other and unto the abundance of life. Being the centre of all creation, he would have been able to direct the whole of creation towards God.

However, after the fall, man lost this state of glory; his heart became hardened and his mind darkened. Death and corruption entered into his nature and he became a slave to sin.

Since man was created to be the centre of creation, this central position continued. Yet, it continued in a negative way, as he led the whole of creation (including himself) to destruction and perishing.

Being in such state, it was not possible for man to discover the mystery of the Hypostases, the hypostatic principle, which exists within him and through which he can be saved from his tragic state.

Yet, through His utter humility and love of

mankind expressed on the cross and also through His resurrection, Jesus, the Son of God bestowed on man *the grace of repentance* and *the power of regeneration* by which the image of God in man can be restored to its original condition.

Through this struggle to restore the divine image, the hypostatic principle develops and is perfected in man.

Man would thus be truly able to restore his real human nature as was created by God.

As a result, man's relationship with God and his fellow-humans would become truly great.

Yet, this spiritual diligence and completing true repentance will not be without pain and suffering. This allows one to enter into the fellowship of Christ's suffering; and hence, get rid of his egoism (which wells out of the poison that has entered through the old serpent); and become united with the Son of God. As a result of this unity, the power of Christ's resurrection flows in him and he bears *'the heavenly image'* (1 Corinthians 15: 45, 49) as he would be born anew of the Spirit!

'And so it is written, "The first man Adam became a living being." The last Adam became a life-giving

spirit… And as we have borne the image of the man of dust, we shall also bear <u>the image of the heavenly Man'</u> (1 Corinthians 15: 45, 49).

When the person is born of the Spirit, the Holy Spirit forms Christ in his heart.

Through humility and repentance, one reaches the point of being *'nobody'*; he gets freed from the law of sin and is able to resist the fallen nature. As a result, he enters into the mystery of the hypostasis, the hypostatic form of being. The hypostasis which was only potential becomes actualised (it becomes a reality) within him. As a result, the Uncreated light shines upon him and grants him the ability to be filled with God, to be able to assimilate the Energy of God's very being.

This in turn binds him to Christ who is the unique centre of the whole creation. He participates in the divine universality of the God-Man; and so, he too becomes great.

Through the strength of the divine love, man embraces the whole world.

What belongs to God by nature, man acquires it by grace.

In this state, the created hypostasis (man as a

person) enters into a more intimate relationship with Christ. From being a slave, he becomes a friend:

'No longer do I call you servants, for a servant does not know what his master is doing; but I have called you friends, for all things that I heard from My Father I have made known to you' (John 15: 15).

Man then begins to work with God in matters that are of cosmic dimension: the salvation of the whole world.

This cosmic person continues to understand God's righteousness more and more and continues to love Him more and more in order to attract God's great mercy upon the earth.

Under these conditions, man's being expands by the work of the Holy Spirit; and his hypostatic principle gets elevated to majestic heights. He thus finds special favour with God and becomes the subject of God's delight: *'this is my beloved son in whom I am well pleased'*. In such state and condition, this person can intercede on behalf of the world.

The Holy Spirit broadens man's heart in a way that makes man able to bear humanity in prayer; the whole human race would be experienced and seen as one man.

In the life of the Holy Trinity, each Hypostasis bears the fullness of the divine Being. Similarly, in the human life, each fulfilled hypostasis (person) bears the whole human race as his own being.

Summary

When man repents, he does not only repent for himself, but he also repents for the whole creation, the whole of Adam.

When man is born again in Spirit (and is victorious like Christ over all evil powers), he is actually being born again into the higher world of the Kingdom of heaven. Therefore, as a true son and heir of God, he raises the whole creation with himself.

Exactly as he was loved by Christ *'unto the end'* (John 13: 1), this person would also love his divine Benefactor to the point of self-denial; counting his soul of no value (Acts 20: 24); being ready for every sacrifice for the sake of God's holy and perfect will.

'But I do not account my life of any value nor as precious to myself, if only I may finish my course and the ministry that I received from the Lord Jesus, to testify to the gospel of the grace of God' (Acts 20: 24).

With the same love, he prays for the whole world.

On that level, the hypostatic principle is realised and actualised in man.

Being united with Christ and through the power of Christ's love, man embraces all things: the heaven and the earth. He follows Christ wherever Christ goes, as written in Revelation 14: 4: *'It is these who follow the Lamb wherever He goes.'*

Part 5:

*The Person of Jesus Christ as God and Saviour**

---

*Ideas and spiritual principles presented in this part are mostly inspired by the book Orthodox Dogmatic Theology by Dumitru Staniloae.

Chapter 1. The Saving Power of the Incarnate God

Sin closes off the human person from God and his neighbour. It also weakens the persona which is the hypostatic character of man; it weakens his loving humanity.

Jesus is absolutely sinless; sin cannot exist in Him. He does not have a human hypostasis that closes itself off from God.

The Divine Word, the Incarnate Jesus, took our nature; hypostasizing our nature in Him and cleansing it of all impurities. He deified it through His incarnation. By this, He has placed our nature in the fullness of freedom from sinful passions.

Christ's humanity is completely open to the Father and to the Holy Spirit; and is also open to its neighbours. The divine Hypostasis has neither enmity towards man nor fear of being limited by man. Therefore, the human nature does not face the problem of being in competition with other humans.

The *divine nature* is united with *the human nature* in the Person of Christ; so that the human nature can participate in the divine nature; and also so that the divine nature may take upon itself the human weaknesses.

In Western theology, there is a tendency to avoid such communication between the two natures: the divine and the human. Western theology tends to only consider that the two natures come in unity in the Person of Christ so that Christ's identity, as man and God, can represent us before God and bear the punishment in our place.

But there is actually much more than that, because through this unity between the two natures, we—as humans—receive and are granted new abilities—as we will explain below.

How was our nature transformed in Christ's Hypostasis, acquiring new abilities?

The human nature bears in it what we call *'the innocent passions'* which are the need to eat, drink, sleep, and the like. Yet, because sin entered into the human nature, the human nature became weak; and hence, these natural needs became uncontrolled.

Jesus came and took our humanity with its characteristics; yet, he strengthened our human nature through His divine nature so that our human nature may acquire the suitable ability of controlling itself.

We notice that when Christ strengthened our nature, He did not wish to strengthen it more than necessary. He still kept a place for human diligence, strengthened by grace, to exercise the required self-control. Yet, He strengthened it to a suitable measure to be able to exercise the required self-control.

Also, because of the sin that has entered the human nature, the human nature became opaque and lost the transparency towards God and others. In His Hypostatic union with our nature, Christ desired to restore to it the ability of being transparent towards God and others; so that, through the work of redemption, it may be able to draw near God and others with spontaneity and transparency, bearing the features of Christ.

This was not without multiplied pain and suffering in the life of Christ due to His natural transparency and His complete openness to God, the Father, and to man. He; therefore, suffered the pain of this opaqueness and closure in order to free man from them. This was not to be achieved without passing through actual death in His human body.

Realising what Christ has done for us, as God and as Saviour, leads us to worship in Spirit and truth:

- In his book *'Adoration in Spirit and Truth'*, St. Cyril of Alexandria (5th century) explains that one can enter God's presence only in a state of pure sacrifice; and no human being can do this on his own because of sin. Christ alone, as man without sin[17], is able to enter into God's presence as a pure sacrifice. It is only in Christ that we can do the same.

If sin is the egoism which is expressed in spiritual pride or the pleasures of the flesh, then, the opposite of sin would be the *perfectly pure sacrifice*.

For this very reason, we worship Christ as the

---

17 Christ is without sin means that He did not commit any personal sin and He also came into existence without original sin.

Lord and Saviour because in Him we can enter into God's presence as worshippers.

- Jesus has sovereignty over all things, but He is also a Lamb slaughtered for us. He is our Master, but He is a Master who touches our hearts by the fact that He became and remains to be a slaughtered Lamb without ceasing to be a Master.

And every creature which is in heaven and on the earth and under the earth and such as are in the sea, and all that are in them, I heard saying: "Blessing and honour and glory and power be to Him who sits on the throne, and to the Lamb, forever and ever" (Revelation 5: 13).

He is the *Lord* because He is the *Lamb* who takes away the sins of the world.

He is the Lamb who takes away the sins of the world because He is the almighty God; but, He is almighty in His love.

He obliges us in our conscience. He draws from us the deepest, willing, and total adoration because He is our most admirable model of a servant:

'And whoever desires to be first among you, let him be your slave—just as the Son of Man did not come to be served, but to serve, and to give His life a ransom for

many' (Matthew 20: 27, 28).

Because of this, we offer Him total adoration accompanied by the deepest love.

The incarnate Son of God revealed to us the mystery of the *serving Lordship* with the apparent paradox of combining the deepest adoration with the warmest love.

There is indeed no contradiction between the true Lordship and service. It is the sin of pride that has separated them and created contradiction between them.

The sin of pride has separated our hearts from God; and so we worship Him out of fear.

Christ has re-established the true worship of God and of Himself by revealing to us the Loving God.

We worship Christ with much love because He became the Son of man; making us His brothers and the children of the Heavenly Father.

Chapter 2. The Work of Salvation

The connection between Christ's Person and His work of salvation is based on the unity of the two natures in His One Person. There is an inseparable bond between His Person and His work of salvation.

Christ's work of salvation *is directed towards His human nature* which He fills with His divinity and liberates from the innocent passions, sufferings, and the death that resulted from the original sin.

Christ's work of salvation *is then directed towards us* in order that we too may liberate ourselves from sin in this life and from the innocent passions, corruptibility, and the death in the life to come.

His work of salvation _is also directed towards God_ in order to glorify Him.

Though Christ's work of salvation has three directions, the work itself is **not divided.**

His work of salvation can be considered from three aspects; but, since it is not divided, each aspect cannot be considered in separation from the other two.

Since Christ exercises these three kinds of activities as aspects of His one work of salvation, He was considered from the very beginning as _High Priest_ (Hebrews 9: 11); as _Teacher-Prophet_; and as Master, Lord, or _King_ (Revelation 12: 10; Revelation 11: 15; Matthew 28: 18).

'But Christ came as High Priest of the good things to come, with the greater and more perfect tabernacle not made with hands, that is, not of this creation' (Hebrews 9:11).

'Then I heard a loud voice saying in heaven, "Now salvation, and strength, and the kingdom of our God, and the power of His Christ have come, for the accuser of our brethren, who accused them before our God day and night, has been cast down' (Revelation 12: 10).

'Then the seventh angel sounded: And there were loud voices in heaven, saying, "The kingdoms of this world have become the kingdoms of our Lord and of His Christ, and He shall reign forever and ever" (Revelation 11: 15).

'And Jesus came and spoke to them, saying, "All authority has been given to Me in heaven and on earth' (Matthew 28: 18).

In His work of salvation, Christ **manifests His threefold relation:** with *His human nature*, with *the Father*, and with *the human beings*. Through this work, He **manifests His threefold ministry** as: *Teacher-Prophet, High Priest*, and *King*.

Through these three operations or qualities (Teacher-Prophet, High Priest, and King), He can save human beings and make them perfect.

A. Jesus Christ the Prophet and Teacher

Jesus Christ is the supreme Teacher and Prophet through His Own Person. This means that He is the Teacher and the Prophet by Himself not through a gift.

His teaching shows the true path to eternity.

But He, Himself, being the path towards perfection

and also perfection itself, showed us the ultimate model for humankind.

We learn by looking at His Person and can follow in his footsteps by being in close contact and communication with Him: *'learn from Me, for I am gentle and lowly in heart'* (Matthew 11: 29).

He is the Teacher and the Prophet because He is not only man, but also God. In this sense, His teaching is the ultimate revelation about God and about man.

In Him, all prophecies are fulfilled.

The prophets of the Old Testament communicated a partial truth about God and about man. They could not have the whole truth in themselves because they were not able to fully identify with the truth they communicated. They could not communicate this truth with the full power which would transform others.

Christ's teaching is totally different from this. In every word He says, one feels the wholeness of the living truth which is identical with His Person.

Christ and the Kingdom of God

Christ announced the coming of the Kingdom of God in order to help people believe in Him. The

Kingdom of God began from the moment of Christ's appearance in the midst of mankind.

Christ is the King and the Kingdom is in Him. Therefore, when He preaches about the Kingdom, His Person is revealed. His preaching and teaching revealed His Person.

This Kingdom began in its fullness at the time of His resurrection.

His teaching in relation to the Law

As Jacob, the Patriarch, unpeeled the twigs (Genesis 30: 37), Christ uncovers the meaning of the Law. In this context, St. Cyril of Alexandria writes: *'He unpeels the Law of its shadow and eliminates the cover from the writings of the prophets.'*[18]

Moses was unable to lift up the people to the mountain of the infinite and direct knowledge of God, but Christ can do so. St. Cyril says: *'the mountain is interpreted as being 'the knowledge of Christ's mystery'...Moses brought the people close to the mountain, but did not take them up.'*[19]

To sum up:

Christ's teaching is one of the forms through which the Person of Christ is *communicated* through

---

[18] Cyril of Alexandria, Glaphyra
[19] Ibid

His human nature to other human persons for their salvation.

Christ's words and deeds are necessary for knowing His Person as God and as man. This is because the Person cannot be known except through words and deeds.

Christ is present where His words and deeds are remembered with faith in Him.

All His words have full backing in His Person. His words are manifested and incarnated in His life.

In His teaching, Christ unceasingly communicated His supreme love; and He requires a corresponding response of love from the human person.

The purpose of all the teaching He gives us is to make us respond to God's call.

B. Jesus Christ the High Priest and Supreme Sacrifice

As explained above, Christ's ministry as Teacher-Prophet is mainly _directed to us_.

His ministry as High-Priest—through which He offers Himself as a Sacrifice—is mainly _directed to the_

Father. Yet, it still comprises the other two elements; namely, being directed *towards Himself* and *towards us*.

In order to have a complete understanding of Christ's sacrifice, we need to see it as being directed *towards God* and also *towards the human nature*. This human nature was taken on by Christ; so the sacrifice is directed *to Him;* and then, through Him, *towards human beings*. Through the sacrifice of Himself, Christ was restoring and renewing the human nature. He first restored it in Himself (in His human nature); and then through Him in all who believe in Him.

The human person cannot come out of the state of enmity to God except through sacrifice. Yet, it is a sacrifice that the human person cannot offer; but, only Christ can.

Christ, as a man, gains God's love for human nature by correcting and amending this state of enmity towards God, through sacrifice. On the other hand, through sacrifice, Christ manifests the will to be totally dedicated to God; and hence, the human nature is restored from its state of sickness. These are *two inseparable aspects* of sacrifice.

In short, sacrifice allows the restoration of the communion between God and man. The restoration of communion means that the human nature is healed from its egoism; and at the same time, God's love to man is manifested through His will to adorn the human person with His gifts.

The content of this sacrifice and its significance for humanity

Christ's death, as a sacrifice directed toward God—with its great effect on His humanity—is an expression of the **total surrender** of Christ, as a man, to the Father.

Also, we can say that the cause of suffering in the sacrifice, regarding its relation to human persons, is Christ's deep and **total compassion** for humans.

This compassion, which went all the way to death, can now impart to human beings the ability to crucify their egoism, by taking strength from Christ's death.

Christ remains in a great and supreme state of sacrifice in the double sense of His surrender, as a man, to the Father and of His compassion for humans.

Christ's body

Christ's body, as a sacrificed and risen body, has a central importance in our salvation, because it is the body of God, the Word.

His body is filled with the entire divine life and is a ring through which the divine fire is transmitted to us. This fire illuminates, purifies, and deifies us; and it melts away the power of death in us.

We can now understand that the central importance of Christ's body is based on His identification as High Priest and His identity as Sacrifice.

Man was created *to be a Priest* on behalf of the whole creation, offering the praise of creation to the Creator. At the same time, man was created to *be a sacrifice*, offering himself to God.

Therefore, when the Word, the Logos, was incarnated and accepted to become man, He naturally became the Priest and the Sacrifice—because this is God's mind towards man in general.

Christ offered His body as a sacrifice; and at the same time, He is the Priest who offered the sacrifice of Himself. By His death and resurrection, His body became the seed of resurrection offered to man. Christ became the first-fruit of all creation; all are in Him and He is the Head of the body.

'And He is before all things, and in Him all things consist. And He is the head of the body, the church, who

is the beginning, the firstborn from the dead, that in all things He may have the pre-eminence' (Colossians 1: 17, 18).

'But now Christ is risen from the dead, and has become the first fruits of those who have fallen asleep. For since by man came death, by Man also came the resurrection of the dead. For as in Adam all die, even so in Christ all shall be made alive' (1 Corinthians 15: 20 – 22).

Exactly as Christ expressed His love for man through offering Himself as a Sacrifice—both as the Priest and the Slain, man—being a priest—is also called to offer himself as a sacrifice to God in response to the love offered to him through the Person of Christ, the Priest and the Slain.

Neglecting our *priesthood* responsibility (as priests in Christ, according to Revelation 1: 6) is considered negligence of the humility and ministry which we should offer to the Lord.

This in itself hinders the work of sanctification in us because sanctification is associated with the holy sacrifice of Christ which sanctifies us and makes us holy.

Also, neglecting to offer ourselves as a *sacrifice* to God hinders our boldness and our access to the

Father. Because this sacrifice is made holy by the sacrifice of Christ, it brings us to the Father in Christ: *'For through Him we both have access by one Spirit to the Father'* (Ephesians 2: 18); and it is also written: *'in whom we have boldness and access with confidence through faith in Him'* (Ephesians 3: 12).

Finally, Christ's body (His flesh) is an eternal sacrifice which instils in us and imparts to us the spirit of sacrifice. It is also the place where all the glory and divine power, which is intended for us, dwells.

Christ's sacrifice as a means to conquer death

According to St. Gregory of Nyssa, death took place because of the separation between the body and the soul as a result of the separation of man from God. This is because the relationship between man and God provides the cohesive force between the body and the soul.

According to the divine economy, Christ accepted death (the separation between the body and the soul); so that by His resurrection and through His humanity, man can restore the ability to regain the cohesive force between the soul and the body.

Thus, Christ conquered death by His death. He annulled the effect of death which separates the body from the soul. Through this, we receive this result of annulling the effect of death. This is the basis of the resurrection which will be for humanity. Because of this, we also see that Christ allowed death to separate the body and the soul, but He did not allow it to make the body decompose and decay. This is because of the divine economy to annul this separation between the body and the soul and account this for every believer.

St. Gregory of Nyssa (4th century) writes:

'He knitted together again the disunited elements, cementing them, as it were, together with the cement of His Divine power, and recombining what has been severed in a union never to be broken. And this is the resurrection.'[20]

Another important point:

Christ enters with His sacrifice in the Holy of Holies on high; He remains there for eternity; and He makes us partakers of His glory:

'Who being the brightness of His glory and the express image of His person, and upholding all things by the word of His power, when He had by Himself purged our sins, sat down at the right hand of the Majesty on high' (Hebrews 1: 3).

'But this Man, after He had offered one sacrifice for sins

---

[20] Gregory of Nyssa, The Great Catechism

forever, sat down at the right hand of God' (Hebrews 10: 12).

When we die to ourselves, we are united through love with the One who died to Himself for the Father and for all mankind. Christ remains eternally alive before the Father; and we, too, remain eternally in Him.

St. Cyril of Alexandria (5th centuries) writes:

'By shedding His own blood for us, thus putting an end to death and corruption, our Lord Jesus Christ makes us His own as the ones who no longer live our life, but His. His very death was an act of victory over death.'[21]

Therefore, when we die, at the end of our life, it is not a punishment because this purpose of death was removed and abolished in Christ's death—for those who are united with Him.

Yet, we die to the old man; namely, to sin. We then need to sanctify ourselves through the power of the sanctified body of Christ of whom we partake. We do so by fighting our sinful passions and bearing without sin the innocent passions; or, by accepting sufferings peacefully and submissively knowing that they are consequences of sin.

---

21 Cyril of Alexandria, Glaphyra

'For if we have been united together in the likeness of His death, certainly we also shall be in the likeness of His resurrection, knowing this, that our old man was crucified with Him, that the body of sin might be done away with, that we should no longer be slaves of sin' (Romans 6: 5, 6).

'I beseech you therefore, brethren, by the mercies of God, that you present your bodies a living sacrifice, holy, acceptable to God, which is your reasonable service' (Romans 12: 1).

Our priestly vocation

In man's role as a priest, the first thing that he needs to offer to God as a sacrifice is himself not the world.

Apostle Peter links *'the royal priesthood'* of those who believe in Christ to their duty to proclaim in their being *'the praises of Him who called you out of darkness into His marvellous light'* and to *'abstain from fleshly lusts which war against the soul'.*

'But you are a chosen generation, a royal priesthood, a holy nation, His own special people, that you may proclaim the praises of Him who called you out of darkness into His marvellous light...Beloved, I beg you

as sojourners and pilgrims, abstain from fleshly lusts which war against the soul' (1 Peter 2: 9, 11).

We can enter to the Father and have communion with Him only when we become holy sacrifices. But, it is only in Christ that we can enter into this communion with the Father.

In such a way, we continue our priestly vocation properly and in a way that pleases the Father.

C. Jesus, a Risen Lord and King

Not only is Jesus a Teacher-Prophet and a High Priest-Sacrifice; but, He is also a King.

He is not only a King as God since the creation of the world; but, He also has this royal rank as man.

The Lord Himself acknowledged before Pilate that He is King (John 18: 36; Matthew 27:11; Mark 15: 2; Luke 23: 3).

Jesus answered, 'My kingdom is not of this world. If My kingdom were of this world, My servants would fight, so that I should not be delivered to the Jews; but now My kingdom is not from here' (John 18: 36).

Now Jesus stood before the governor. And the governor asked Him, saying, "Are You the King of the Jews?" Jesus said to him, "It is as you say" (Matthew 27:11).

Then Pilate asked Him, "Are You the King of the Jews?"
He answered and said to him, "It is as you say" (Mark
15: 2).

Then Pilate asked Him, saying, "Are You the King of
the Jews?" He answered him and said, "It is as you say"
(Luke 23: 3).

The gospel mentions that this authority is
manifested in His teaching: *'for He taught them as one*
having authority, and not as the scribes' (Matthew 7:
29).

It is evident here that Jesus as man had royal
power before the resurrection.

This authority was also clear in His miracles of
healing; it was clear over nature, and also over the
souls of those who heard Him, whether the disciples
or those around Him, when He gave them His
commandments; or even, when He rebuked them for
their lack of faith.

The authority of Christ exercised over the souls
was not only the authority of His divine glory, but also
the authority of love which is in harmony with His
kenosis.

Jesus said before Pilate that His Kingdom is not of
this world. This means that it is not like the kingdoms

of this world, because He captured the hearts of people through love, service, and sacrifice:

'For even the Son of Man did not come to be served, but to serve, and to give His life a ransom for many' (Mark 10: 45).

Through His resurrection, Christ is raised to full royal authority so that this may also be manifested in: His Ascension; sitting at the right hand of the Father; leading the work of salvation; the Second Coming in glory; and the Last Judgment.

After resurrection, Jesus said: *'All authority has been given to Me in heaven and on earth'* (Matthew 28: 18). Also, Apostle Paul wrote: *'Therefore God also has highly exalted Him and given Him the name which is above every name'* (Philippians 2: 9).

Christ does not keep this glory—to which He is raised —to Himself; He spreads it over us because He has received it for us.

The authority which Christ gives us helps us in overcoming sin and controlling the blameless passions so that they would not become sins.

The acts by which the incarnated Christ manifests His full royal authority

1. The Resurrection of Christ

2. The Ascension into heaven and the sitting at the right hand of the Father

1. The Resurrection of Christ

• The reality of resurrection

According to Apostle Paul, the resurrection is not a simple return of life to the body. It is also not a creation of a new body out of nothing. It is a radical transformation of the mortal body through an act of creation performed upon that body.

Apostle Paul speaks of *Christ's pneumatisation.*

Pneumatisation is the process of transformation from the merely bodily form to the *'spiritual body'*, as Paul calls it in 1 Corinthians 15: 44:

'It is sown a natural body, it is raised a spiritual body. There is a natural body, and there is a <u>spiritual body.</u>'

The term comes from the Greek word *'pneuma'* which means *'spirit'. Pneumatised* means *to become spiritual.*

So, Christ's pneumatisation is the effect of the Holy Spirit's most intensive work in Christ's body that gives it transparency and makes it illuminate with light and glory.

In this context, Apostle Paul writes:

'Therefore, from now on, we regard no one according to the flesh. Even though we have known Christ according to the flesh, yet now we know Him thus no longer' (2 Corinthians 5: 16).

'But we all, with unveiled face, beholding as in a mirror the glory of the Lord, are being transformed into the same image from glory to glory, just as by the Spirit of the Lord' (2 Corinthians 3: 18).

This work of the Spirit is also sanctifying. This sanctification does not take place when one does not make an effort toward purification from pleasures which cause the body to become dense and when one does not renounce the ego. In Christ, self-renunciation went all the way to the acceptance of death.

Apostle Paul says that the resurrected body is a spiritual body which penetrates and changes its mode of existence.

'It is sown a natural body, it is raised a spiritual body. There is a natural body, and there is a spiritual body' (1 Corinthians 15: 44).

- ## Resurrection and history

Christ established a certain connection with history. He has brought certain effects into history in order to liberate history from the dominion of death.

Resurrection has taken a historical Person, Christ, out of the present realm of existence; and hence, opened the way for the liberation of the whole of history from this physical existence.

History, is meant to be raised to a superior level and existence, to the level of the incorruptible and eternal life, to the spiritualised realm of existence. In this realm of existence, it is not the uniform process of nature that reigns, but the freedom of the human spirit, through which the Holy Spirit makes the body spiritual and transparent.

- **The spiritual radiance and the transforming effect of Christ's resurrection on the world**

In Eastern thought, Christ's Cross itself is victorious. This is because after Christ's death, His soul which is full of the Godhead went into hell/hades, where it could not be held. This soul which is full of the Godhead conquered hades/hell; and then it raised His body as well; His body did not lack the Godhead and was not abandoned to corruption.

In the New Testament, there are some references that speak about the Father raising the Son. Examples of these are: Acts 2: 24, 32; Acts 3: 15; Acts 5: 30; Acts 13: 37; Acts 17: 31; Romans 4: 24; Romans 8: 11;

Romans 10: 9; 1 Corinthians 6: 14; 1 Corinthians 15: 15; 2 Corinthians 4: 14; Galatians 1: 1; Colossians 2: 12; 1 Thessalonians 1: 10.

'whom God raised up, having loosed the pains of death, because it was not possible that He should be held by it...This Jesus God has raised up, of which we are all witnesses' (Acts 2: 24, 32).

These references in the New Testament made some theologians teach that Jesus was helpless in His death and that the Father raised Him.

However, the New Testament does not present Jesus only as an object of the resurrection, but Jesus is also presented ***as the subject*** of the act of resurrection—as we read in many references.

Examples of these references are:

Matthew 16: 21; Matthew 17: 23; Matthew 20: 19; Mark 9: 31; Luke 18: 33; Luke 24: 34; John 2: 22; 1 Corinthians 15: 4, 12, 16, 17; 2 Corinthians 5: 15; 1 Thessalonians 4: 14; 2 Timothy 2: 8.

'And deliver Him to the Gentiles to mock and to scourge and to crucify. And the third day He will rise again' (Matthew 20: 19).

Actually, the Father, the Son, and the Holy Spirit are

all cooperatively involved in the act of resurrection.

St. Cyril of Alexandria says: *'By being the might of God the Father, the Son Himself has made His body alive.'*[22]

According to the Church fathers, Christ deified the body, even during the course of His earthly life; He filled the body with the power to remain pure.

In death, Christ's body could not be emptied of this deification. So, Christ's resurrection was prepared by this union of His humanity with the Godhead, through His divine Hypostasis—which also bore the human nature.

Therefore, Christ's risen body is a source of divine life for us in our earthly life; it is a source of strength and purity. And of course, it is also a guarantee given to us by the Father so that we, too, will rise again.

In the writings of the early Church, we read about the effect of Christ's risen body on us.

St. Cyril of Alexandria wrote:

For Christ has risen, destroying death, to save us from corruption and to persuade us, by eliminating the grief caused by it, to joyfully shout: "You have turned my mourning into dancing"[23] *(Psalm 30: 11).*

---

22 Cyril of Alexandria, Glaphyra
23 Ibid

- **Resurrection began with Christ's descent to hell**

When Christ descended into hell/hades, His soul could not be held there. His soul is the first soul that could not be held in hell. In 1 Peter 3: 19, we read: *'by whom also He went and <u>preached to the spirits</u> in prison'.*

Christ was also able to liberate from hell the souls of those who had believed in the promises of His Coming—which were foretold in the Old Testament.

Writing about the dominion obtained by Christ over the faithful souls of those in hell, St. Cyril says: *'It is for this Christ died and rose again; so that, He might rule over the dead as well'*[24] (Romans 14: 9).

'For to this end Christ died and rose and lived again, that He might be Lord of both the dead and the living' (Romans 14: 9).

The moment Christ descended into hell was the beginning of His resurrection. He was still dead in the body, *'but made alive by the Spirit'* (1 Peter 3: 18). This was also the beginning of His royal dominion, being the King.

Now, we can understand that the words:

---

24 Ibid

'preached to the spirits' (1 Peter 3: 19) refer to Christ's announcement to them of their liberation and the future resurrection of the body. He brought to them the great news of salvation which He has accomplished.

Christ first conquered hell with His soul which is united with His divine Hypostasis. Then, this soul which is filled with the Holy Spirit irradiated power unto the souls of those in hell—the souls who had hoped in Him. It was a power that liberated them from the dominion of hell.

Based on this, we notice that the Western icons of resurrection depict Christ rising alone; while the eastern icons depict Him rising and lifting up with Him Adam and Eve from hell in order to reveal the aspect of His redeeming work.

• Encounters with the Risen Lord

All the accounts of those to whom the risen Christ appeared tell of His appearances as *encounters*. He was always the one who took the initiative of the meeting. Be it a word, a sign, a greeting, a blessing, an address, a message, a teaching, a consolation, a sending, it was always a free gift. In those encounters Christ was revered and worshiped as God, for the first time:

'And as they went to tell His disciples, behold, Jesus met them, saying, "Rejoice!" So they came and held Him by the feet and <u>worshiped Him</u>...When they saw Him, they <u>worshiped Him</u>; but some doubted' (Matthew 28: 9, 17).

And Thomas answered and said to Him, "My Lord <u>and my God!</u>" (John 20: 28).

It was only after the resurrection of Christ that the disciples fully understood and perceived the teaching of Jesus which He had taught them before the resurrection and comprehended the references to Him in the Old Testament. They started to see that everything in the Old Testament is linked to Jesus and refers to Him. From that point onwards, when they preach, they will refer to the Old Testament as leading to Christ.

These encounters determined the beginning of the *mission* of the disciples. Christ sent them with a power to which they could not respond with indifference. He sent them to the whole world because Christ has dominion over all:

So Jesus said to them again, 'Peace to you! As the Father has sent Me, <u>I also send you</u>' (John 20: 21).

'And Jesus came and spoke to them, saying, "All authority has been given to Me in heaven and on earth.

Go *therefore and make disciples <u>of all the nations</u>, baptizing them in the name of the Father and of the Son and of the Holy Spirit, teaching them to observe all things that I have commanded you; and lo, I am with you always, even to the end of the age." Amen'* (Matthew 28: 18 – 20).

'And that repentance and remission of sins should be preached in His name <u>to all nations</u>, beginning at Jerusalem. And you are witnesses of these things. Behold, I send the Promise of My Father upon you; but tarry in the city of Jerusalem until you are endued with power from on high' (Luke 24: 47 – 49).

'But you <u>shall receive power</u> when the Holy Spirit has come upon you; and you shall be witnesses to Me in Jerusalem, and in all Judea and Samaria, and <u>to the end of the earth</u>' (Acts 1: 8).

- **The power of the Lord's risen body**

The power of the Lord's risen body continued to be communicated to the disciples and to all those who believe in Him even after Christ's ascension into Heaven.

Through the power of Christ's death and resurrection we die to sin; but, we are made alive for God:

'And if Christ is in you, the body is dead because of sin, but the Spirit is life because of righteousness. But if the Spirit of Him who raised Jesus from the dead dwells in you, He who raised Christ from the dead will also give life to your mortal bodies through His Spirit who dwells in you' (Romans 8: 10, 11).

The body of the risen Christ is filled with holiness and deification. This holiness, transparency, and deification are communicated to us through His Spirit.

- **The wounds of Christ**

These wounds are not just memories (they are not something that happened in the past and is over), but they are a permanent existing reality in Christ. In other words, their work and effect is constant and continues in Christ, for our sake.

These wounds are the source and well of Christ's sacrificial act, His death. If we draw from this well when we worship the Father, the sweet aroma of these wounds extends in us and fills us, replacing the rotten fragrance of sin.

In this respect, St. Cyril of Alexandria writes:

'There is no doubt that sin exists in us as a sad state with a bad fragrance. The sad and foul smell is

transformed through Christ into joy. Through faith, Christ transmits a sweet fragrance to the human person. We offer ourselves to God through Christ, for He is the one who purifies sinners by His sacrifice and washes spiritually the unclean.'

'Through Christ, we also offer ourselves (to God); and in Him (Christ) we, the unclean, have the courage to approach. But, we approach through faith; and we offer ourselves to the Father as a sweet fragrance only if we cease to exist for ourselves, if we only have Christ in us as a spiritual sweet fragrance.'[25]

- **Unity with Christ and its fruits**

a. Broadness in life and in knowledge

This unity and intimacy with Christ allows us to enter into the fellowship of the life of Christ. This, in turn, broadens our constrictions and alters our limited knowledge of God.

St. Cyril of Alexandria writes:

'Those who are in intimacy with the Son receive through the Spirit a broadening of their life and knowledge from the largeness of Christ's life as a man, advancing toward the spiritual stature of Christ (Ephesians 4: 13).'[26]

---

25 Cyril of Alexandria, Adoration in Spirit
26 Ibid

'Till we all come to the unity of the faith and of the knowledge of the Son of God, to a perfect man, to the measure of the stature of the fullness of Christ' (Ephesians 4: 13).

St. Cyril then continues:

'Together with Christ, who ascended through sacrifice and resurrection, we ascend to the peaks of the knowledge of God and of divine life through purification from selfish passions.'[27]

b.   How does the Father see us?

Christ presents—in Himself—to the Father all those who believe in Him; therefore, those believers are attached to Christ. They are seen in Him by the Father, but He also has them inscribed in His eternal memory and remembrance as we read in Psalm 112: 6: *'The righteous will be in everlasting remembrance'*. The Father sees them in Christ's memory and remembrance.

At the same time, the Father sees Christ imprinted in the believers in His state of Sacrifice and Resurrection.

The Father sees in Christ's face all those who believe in Him. At the same time, the Father sees

---

27 Cyril of Alexandria, Glaphyra

Christ imprinted in the face of every believer.

c.   How are we going to see Him when He comes again in His glory?

When Christ returns, in His Second Coming, the economy of incarnation will have ended, because at that time we shall see Him in His divine glory.

His body will not cease to exist, but it will be transparent, and, through it, we will directly see God in glory.

In this context, St. Cyril writes:

'When He will come in the glory of the Father, we will no longer offer our due confession about His passion because we will know Him clearly: 'face to face', as God.'[28]

The economy (oikonomia) by which He became incarnate has passed. The reason for the incarnation will cease and a greater knowledge will come about. There will be brightness, vision, and understanding of the glorious salvation coming to us from Him.

'For now we see in a mirror dimly, but then face to face. Now I know in part; then I shall know fully, even as I have been fully known' (1 Corinthians 13: 12).

---

28 Ibid

'Beloved, now we are children of God; and it has not yet been revealed what we shall be, but we know that when He is revealed, we shall be like Him, for we shall see Him as He is' (1 John 3: 2).

2. The Ascension into heaven and the sitting at the right Hand of the Father

According to the epistle to the Hebrews, Jesus Christ presents Himself with His sacrifice before the Father; and then, He sits at His right Hand. His sacrifice has an eternal power to purify those who believe.

'Who being the brightness of His glory and the express image of His person, and upholding all things by the word of His power, when He had by Himself purged our sins, sat down at the right hand of the Majesty on high, having become so much better than the angels, as He has by inheritance obtained a more excellent name than they' (Hebrews 1: 3, 4).

'Therefore He is also able to save to the uttermost those who come to God through Him, since He always lives to make intercession for them' (Hebrews 7:25).

'For a testament is in force after men are dead, since it has no power at all while the testator lives. Therefore

not even the first covenant was dedicated without blood. For when Moses had spoken every precept to all the people according to the law, he took the blood of calves and goats, with water, scarlet wool, and hyssop, and sprinkled both the book itself and all the people, saying, "This is the blood of the covenant which God has commanded you." Then, likewise he sprinkled with blood both the tabernacle and all the vessels of the ministry. And according to the law almost all things are purified with blood, and without shedding of blood there is no remission. Therefore it was necessary that the copies of the things in the heavens should be purified with these, but the heavenly things themselves with better sacrifices than these. For Christ has not entered the holy places made with hands, which are copies of the true, but into heaven itself, now to appear in the presence of God for us' (Hebrews 9: 17 – 24).

'But this Man, after He had offered one sacrifice for sins forever, sat down at the right hand of God' (Hebrews 10: 12).

We see the same thing in the book of Revelation. Christ is the slain Lamb; He is the Sacrifice which has a continual act and effect. But, at the same time, He also reigns:

'Saying with a loud voice: "Worthy is the Lamb who was slain to receive power and riches and wisdom,

and strength and honour and glory and blessing"
(Revelation 5: 12).

According to the New Testament, Christ raises
His humanity to the fullness of power through which
He works upon us in the four successive movements:
the descent into hell; the resurrection with the body;
the ascension into heaven; and the sitting at the right
Hand of the Father.

Through Ascension, He is no more visible; but,
dwells invisibly in those who believe in Him.

This dwelling is _a presence of spiritual depth and
height_ that can be manifested in various degrees of
intensity, according to the degree of the spiritual
grasp and/or the level of faith of the person—who
is open to Christ and thus can see or feel Christ in
himself. Those who feel Christ's presence feel it
not just within themselves, but also in others; and
sometimes around them or everywhere.

For the Christians of the early centuries, the
Ascension of Christ's body into heaven is our
ascension, the ascension from our passions in unity
with Him.

- **1 Corinthians 15: 28**

'Now when all things are made subject to Him, then

the Son Himself will also be subject to Him who put all things under Him, that God may be all in all.'

What do these words mean?

In His Ascension and sitting at the right Hand of the Father, Christ reigns as a man filled with infinite divine power and glory. Yet, He reigns with humility and love to mankind; viewing them as His brethren whom He desires to lift up with Him to the same glory: *'And the glory which You gave Me I have given them, that they may be one just as We are one'* (John 17: 22).

When this economy accomplishes its purpose, Jesus as man will also bring to an end His royal ministry, making all things subject to the Father, because all who believe will have become co-kings with Him. This means that they will have reached the glory of perfect freedom in the loving relationship with Christ.

Part 6

The Person of the Holy Spirit

Chapter 1. The Holy Spirit and the Church

- ## The Holy Spirit and Christ working together

The descent of the Holy Spirit gives the Church a real existence; it initiates the indwelling of Christ in human beings; and this in turn initiates the Church.

Therefore, the descent of the Holy Spirit allows the saving work of Christ to extend from His humanity to other human beings.

Through the Incarnation, Crucifixion, Resurrection, and Ascension, Christ lays the foundation of the Church in His own body. Thus, we can say that the Church existed in Christ's body in a potential form.

We should not forget that the Son of God did not become man for Himself; but, so that He could extend salvation, as divine life, from His body to us. The Church is this divine life which has extended from Christ's body into those who believe.

Therefore, the Church existed potentially in Christ's body; she came into life through the Holy Spirit—who has shone forth from the body of Christ into human beings.

This shining forth began at Pentecost when the Holy Spirit descended upon the apostles and made them the first members of the Church, the first believers in whom the power of Christ's pneumatised body extended.

Through the Holy Spirit, Christ penetrates human hearts because Christ's body was made spiritual in an incomparable way through the Spirit.

The presence of the Spirit in us is so connected to the presence of the Son and the presence of the Father that *'no one can say that Jesus is Lord except by the Holy Spirit'* (1 Corinthians 12: 3b).

Also, without the Holy Spirit, we cannot call God as Father (Galatians 4: 6; Romans 8: 15) or even pray *'our Father'*.

Another fact that highlights the indissoluble union between the Spirit's and the Son's presence and work within us is that the Spirit's work consists in fashioning us more and more in the image of the Son, as adopted sons of the Father. But this means that the Son Himself imprints His Person more deeply in us as an active and effective model. He also imprints His Son's affection for the Father, thus receiving us and bringing us into the same intimacy with the Father.

St. Cyril of Alexandria says:

'Therefore, because the Son dwells in us through His Spirit, we say that we are called to the divine sonship.'[29]

St. Cyril also says:

'Christ has sent us the Comforter from heaven, through whom and in whom Christ is with us and dwells in us.'[30]

The Spirit makes Christ more evident to us *as God* and *as Lord*.

The Spirit comes to us as the bearer of the Father's infinite love for His Son. Through the Son, this infinite love embraces us as well.

Through the work of the Holy Spirit, Christ's presence in us becomes more effective. We sense

---

29 St. Cyril of Alexandria, Dialogue 3 on Holy Trinity
30 St. Cyril of Alexandria, Dialogue 7 on Holy Trinity

this work of the Holy Spirit so intensely. Yet, the Holy Spirit does so, not to make Himself felt more intensely; but, to make the presence of Christ felt even more intensely.

Christ said: *'He* (the Holy Spirit) *will take of what is Mine'* (John 16: 14). Clearly, the Holy Spirit will take from the Christ who continues to actively work with Him.

• **The Church and the Holy Spirit**

The Church receives her real existence through the descent of the Holy Spirit because at this point Christ has descended for the first time in the human heart. He is on the divine throne with the Father and at the same time in the hearts of those who believe and in the communion of the believers, the Church. So, Christ is both on the divine throne and He comes continuously from the throne to those who believe.

That is why the Church has the Spirit constantly; and at the same time should ask for Him constantly. She asks for Him because she has Him. The Spirit gives her the strength to ask for Him through prayer, so that He may continue to come more and more:

'Likewise the Spirit also helps in our weaknesses. For we do not know what we should pray for as we ought, but the Spirit Himself makes intercession for us with

groanings which cannot be uttered' (Romans 8: 26).

We can thus see that the Church comes into existence and is maintained through the Holy Spirit, who has descended at Pentecost and remains in the Church.

The Spirit also comes continuously to the Church when she seeks Him through prayer and avoiding sin.

Similarly, Christ is in the Church; He remains and grows in her; or rather, the Church grows in Him. This also takes place and continues to be so through prayer and avoiding sin.

When the Holy Spirit and Christ are present and indwelling, there is always life.

They constantly exhort the human hearts to ask for them so that they would continue to come more and more.

If someone does not live a life of faith, the indwelling of the Spirit and Christ would have a static character; it would be a potential rather than a living actualised experience.

The Holy Spirit and Christ, who remain and grow in the Church and in the believers, are not static. This is because they are not impersonal powers, but

Persons. Persons are always in motion and always want to communicate themselves even more.

The divine Persons come and remain willingly in the believers and the Church; they come and remain in order to come in a higher degree and thus maintain and increase the living communion. Those to whom they come must prepare themselves for this communion by asking and wanting this increased coming of the divine Persons.

- ### *'Tongues of fire'* and a *'sound from heaven'*

The descent of the Spirit in the form of *tongues of fire* signifies that the will of Christ does not only encompass the entire world (unified in His love) within the Church and within His love; but it also preserves the identity of each person in this unity. Christ and the Spirit do not destroy the variety of creation.

St. John Chrysostom says:

'A new and amazing thing has happened: as then (at the tower of Babel) the various tongues divided the world, so now the tongues have united it and have brought into harmony (in a symphony) the things divided.'[31]

For this very reason, the tongues have the form of

---

31 St. John Chrysostom-Homily 2 on Holy Pentecost

fire. The fire burns everything that is evil; everything that divides; it sustains the eagerness and fervour of love towards God and towards others; and it sustains the zeal to spread this love to all people so that all may gather in it.

Not only did the Holy Spirit descend in the form of tongues of fire; but the descent was also accompanied by a sound from heaven: *'And suddenly there came a sound from heaven, as of a rushing mighty wind, and it filled the whole house where they were sitting'* (Acts 2: 2). This means that the Church was born as a reality, not out of a limited and temporary power in the world, but out of a power from heaven that she will bear in herself and communicate to the world.

This was a reality and a communion that represented *'heaven on earth'*; the incarnate Word dwelled in her with His continuously deifying and unifying power.

Chapter 2. The Holy Spirit and His Mystical Work

A. The Work of the Holy Spirit: Divine Grace

The Holy Spirit unites *Christ with human persons* and *human persons with Christ.* Thus, the Spirit is the *sanctifying*, *life-giving*, and *unifying* power in the Church.

He descended at Pentecost giving real existence to the Church. He remains continuously in the Church through an unending shining forth from Christ. He sustains the existence of the Church by bringing new members into her, uniting them in Christ, and giving them new life, the divine life from Christ's life: *'and <u>gave Him to be head</u> over all things to the church, which is His body, the <u>fullness of Him</u> who fills all in all'* (Ephesians 1: 22b, 23).

It is therefore, clear that the Church is founded on a two-fold divine economy: *the work of Christ* and *the work of the Holy Spirit*. The Church is *body* in so far as Christ is her *head*; she is *fullness* in so far as the Holy Spirit fills her with *divinity*.

St. Irenaeus (2nd century) says: *'where the Church is, there is the Spirit; where the Spirit is, there is the Church.'[32]*

- ### The work of Christ and the work of the Spirit go hand in hand

The work of Christ is related to the *human nature* which He recapitulates in His hypostasis.

The work of the Holy Spirit is related to the *persons*. He imports to each one, singly and uniquely, the fullness of deity that is appropriate to every person created in the image of God.

Christ lends His hypostasis to the human nature; and the Holy Spirit gives His divinity to the persons.

Thus, the work of Christ *unifies* and the work of the Holy Spirit *diversifies*. Yet, the one is impossible without the other.

- ### The Holy Spirit is the main Charisma that releases the different gifts

---

32 St. Irenaeus, Against Heresies

According to the early fathers, the Holy Spirit is the main Charisma, the gift of the Father to the person who has become united to Christ. Out of Him, all the other gifts overflow.

*'There are <u>diversities of gifts</u> (charisma), but <u>the same Spirit</u>. There are <u>differences of ministries</u> (diakonia), but the <u>same Lord</u>. And there are <u>diversities of activities</u> (energema which means energies), but it is the <u>same God</u> **who works all in all**. But the manifestation of the Spirit is given to each one for the profit of all'* (1 Corinthians 12: 4 – 7).

We notice three things in this passage:

- o **Gifts** (Charisma) which the **Holy Spirit** distributes and regulates.

- o **Ministries** (Diakonia) which **the Lord** (Kurios, Christ the Lord) distributes and regulates.

- o **Works** (Energma) which **God** (Theos—a general term that refers to the Father, the Godhead) distributes and regulates.

In verse 7, we read: *'But the manifestation of the Spirit is given to each one for the profit of all'*. This is followed by the nine gifts of the Spirit which are: *the word of wisdom, the word of knowledge, faith, gifts of healings, the working of miracles, prophecy, discerning of spirits, different kinds of tongues*, and the *interpretation of tongues* (verses 8, 9). We notice that before listing these gifts, the Scriptures mention the phrase: *'the manifestation of the Spirit is for the profit of all'.* It is therefore clear that these gifts are manifestations of the work of the Holy Spirit.

The word *'manifestation'* is *'phanerosis'* in its Greek origin which signifies *'exhibition'* and *'expression'*.

A Patristic principle related to the work of the Holy Spirit:

The saving work of the Spirit is effective through the divine grace. In other words: *the saving work is divine grace.*

The fathers of the Church specifically highlight that this divine grace emerges from the Hypostases and is inseparable from them. St. Gregory Palamas explains that grace is an uncreated energy which emerges from the divine Being and is not separate from the concerned Hypostasis. This means that during the work of the Hypostasis through His divine grace, the concerned Hypostasis is present. This is because the energy, the divine grace, is the working of the Hypostasis; and there is no work done without the doer of the work.

By understanding grace as divine energy, we

understand that this energy is imprinted on the person in whom the Holy Spirit works. This energy enables the person to cooperate with the Holy Spirit.

This grace or divine energy removes life limitations from our existence. It also opens for us a window towards God, allowing a special kind of communion between the person and God, a communion which quenches the person's thirst.

Through the work of this grace, the person is able to unite with Christ and partake of His holiness.

- **Results of the work of the Holy Spirit**

As the work of the Spirit continues, it produces in the human person a greater power as a permanent state. This in turn bears fruit in that person's life in doing good works, in avoiding sin, in acquiring a state of purity, and in having a more vibrant faith.

So, we can speak of a *state of grace* or the grace that envelops the human person.

With time, the human person is transformed entirely through grace—through the working of the Spirit. This happens if the person cooperates with the Holy Spirit. The person would then bear the *'seal of grace'*—a term used by the fathers of the Church.

St. Symeon speaks of the seal of grace; yet, he prays that Christ does not withdraw it from him:

"You who have shown me Your marvellous glory,
O my God,

And have filled me with Your divine Spirit,
O my Christ,

You have covered me completely
with Your spiritual illumination,

Grant irrevocably Your grace, O my God, to Your
servant; right to the end without diminishment.

Do not withdraw it, O Master;

Do not turn it away, O Creator.

Do not ignore me whom You have placed
before Your face and numbered among
Your servants of light.

You have marked me with Your seal of grace
and claimed me as Your own.[33]

These wonderful poetic words echo the words of Apostle Paul in Ephesians 1: 13, 14:

---

[33] St. Symeon the New Theologian, Hymn 49

'In Him you also trusted, after you heard the word of truth, the gospel of your salvation; in whom also, having believed, <u>you were sealed with the Holy Spirit</u> of promise, who is the guarantee of our inheritance until the redemption of the purchased possession, to the praise of His glory.'

- ### 'Kenosis' of the Spirit

In His descent at Pentecost, the Holy Spirit did not manifest His Person. He did not come in His own name; but, in the name of the Son to bear witness to the Son.

'But the Helper, the Holy Spirit, whom the Father will <u>send in My name</u>, He will teach you all things, and bring to your remembrance all things that I said to you' (John 14: 26).

'But when the Helper comes, whom I shall send to you from the Father, the Spirit of truth who proceeds from the Father, He will <u>testify of Me</u>' (John 15: 26).

'Nevertheless I tell you the truth. It is to your advantage that I go away; for if I do not go away, the Helper will not come to you; but if I depart, I will send Him to you' (John 16: 7).

'However, when He, the Spirit of truth, has come, He will guide you into all truth; for He will not speak on His own authority, but whatever He hears He will speak;

and He will tell you things to come. He will glorify Me, for He will take of what is Mine and declare it to you. All things that the Father has are Mine. Therefore I said that He will take of Mine and declare it to you' (John 16: 13, 14).

This is similar to the Son who came in the name of the Father to make known the Father:

'Nor have I come of Myself, but He sent Me' (John 8: 42b).

'For I have not spoken on My own authority; but the Father who sent Me gave Me a command, what I should say and what I should speak' (John 12: 49).

We also see how the Spirit descends to our level in order to raise us up to the level of being Christ's partners, to imitate Christ and endlessly receive what belongs to Him.

B. The Human Person's Free Cooperation with Grace (Synergism)

'Synergism' is a well-known principle of the early fathers of the Church. It refers to the cooperation between man's will and the work of the Holy Spirit. The word comes from New Latin *'synergismus'* and from Greek *'sunergos'*: *'syn'* means *'together'* and

'ergon' means *'work or energy'*.

The working of the Spirit within us requires our free cooperation.

The Spirit wants us to accept His working and to make it our own through our will and work.

The Spirit does not force us; He does not nullify our will because free will is a gift that God gave to man when He created him.

Freedom is characteristic of the Spirit: *'Now the Lord is the Spirit; and where the Spirit of the Lord is, there is liberty'* (2 Corinthians 3: 17).

He wants to liberate us from the slavery of the passions and help us to advance in genuine freedom to reach the glorious liberty of the children of God.

'For the law of the Spirit of life in Christ Jesus has made me free from the law of sin and death' (Romans 8: 2).

'Because the creation itself also will be delivered from the bondage of corruption into the glorious liberty of the children of God' (Romans 8: 21).

Yet, the Holy Spirit exposes any kind of fake or false liberty that the ego or the passions seek after.

'As free, yet not using liberty as a cloak for vice, but as

bondservants of God' (1 Peter 2: 16).

'For you, brethren, have been called to liberty; only do not use liberty as an opportunity for the flesh, but through love serve one another' (Galatians 5: 13).

In this cooperation with the Spirit, the love between us and Him is manifested and grows.

Also, by cooperating with grace, the human person is re-established in his true humanity, in the likeness of Christ.

C. Gifts as Working of the Spirit

There are visible gifts and non-visible gifts of the Spirit. An example of non-visible gifts is *'the forgiveness of sins'*.

In the Old Testament, we witnessed the gifts of the Holy Spirit; for example, the fire of the Lord fell on Elijah's burnt sacrifice (1 Kings 18: 38) and the sun stood still and did not set until Joshua finished the battle (Joshua 10: 12, 13).

In the New Testament, the gifts were given for the manifestation of the Spirit for the profit of all. The Greek word *'energia'* means *'operations'*; the word *'energma'* means *'manifest'*—referring to the effect of the gift on the very life of the person who receives it.

Every gift which is given in the New Testament is actually given for the sake of the ministry. Therefore, if the person uses the gift for his own sake, this hinders his spiritual growth and corrupts the gift—in the sense that this misuse of the gift annuls the true purpose of the gift and causes its work to cease.

Because of this, the early fathers of the Church stressed the importance of receiving the Person of the Holy Spirit who can then release the gifts as He pleases: *'But now God has set the members, each one of them, in the body just as He pleased'* (1 Corinthians 12: 18).

The Holy Spirit can release a certain gift to a person in order to serve a specific need. He can then stop this gift in the life of that person and release to him another gift for a different need. In this case, the glory would go to God alone and the person would be protected from vain glory and from spoiling the work and the purpose of the gift.

The Holy Spirit is also the Spirit of fellowship and communion: *'the grace of the Lord Jesus Christ and the love of God and the fellowship of the Holy Spirit be with you all'* (2 Corinthians 13: 14).

This Spirit of fellowship continues to work in the human person to help him to be open with love unto God and unto others so that the gift may not be a cause of division or fleshly competition; but, would be for the edification of the believers and the unity of the Church of Christ.

Through the gift, the Spirit unites one human person with another because He is the Spirit of all, the Spirit of Communion. He opens one person towards the other and makes them communicate.

The Spirit is the *'link'* of love between each believer and God; and between him and his neighbour; and thus, He helps all to move towards unity.

Chapter 3. The Holy Spirit and Worship

Worship in spirit and truth

'But the hour is coming, and now is, when the true worshipers will worship the Father in spirit and truth; for the Father is seeking such to worship Him. God is Spirit, and those who worship Him must worship in spirit and truth' (John 4: 23, 24).

- **The understanding of the early Church of the *'worship in spirit and truth'*:**

This phrase is important and it reveals the following:

- o   The Father is seeking those who worship Him

because He is pleased and delighted with this kind of relationship. Worshipping the Father is a source of *delight* and *fellowship*.

o Yet, God is Spirit; and so, He seeks those who worship in spirit and truth; otherwise the worship will not enter into His presence; He will not get in touch with it; it will not be fellowship and delight.

o The verse states that *now* is the hour for this kind of worship, in spirit and truth.

Here we ask: *why, now? Why has this become possible now?*

The verse indicates that previously, in the Old Testament, this kind of worship was not available. The people of God worshipped together during occasions and feasts; yet, they were not able to worship in spirit and truth. However, this has become possible and is requested now. Why is that?

It is because Jesus was incarnated and He gave us the ability to do so.

Yet, the question is:

How can this be available for us practically and what is the correct understanding of this matter?

The answer to this question is clear in the same gospel. According to the early fathers, we can find the true explanation and interpretation of every question in the books of the Scriptures themselves.

If we go back to the beginning of this gospel, John 1, we will find a very important revelation that helps us enter into the mystery of the worship in spirit and truth:

*'And **the Word** became flesh and **dwelt among us,** and we beheld His glory, the glory as of the only begotten of the Father, full of grace and truth'* (John1: 14).

The phrase *'dwelt among us'* which means *'pitched His tent'* reads more accurately, according to the Greek origin, *'tabernacled'*. Also the preposition *'en'* does not only mean *'among us'*; but, it also means *'in us'*. So, according to the Greek origin, the phrase reads: *'**tabernacled in us'**.*

Therefore, in this verse, we can see the ***divine nature*** (the Word, the divine Person of Christ) and the ***human nature*** (His tabernacle).

In this *tabernacle*, the fullness of the *Godhead* dwelt: *'For in Him dwells all the fullness of the Godhead bodily'* (Colossians 2: 9).

The Apostle continues to say: *'we beheld His glory,*

the glory as of the only begotten of the Father'.

This clearly shows that Apostle John had in mind the parallel picture of the Old Testament where the glory of God filled the tabernacle and the temple:

'Then the cloud covered the tabernacle of meeting, and <u>the glory of the Lord filled the tabernacle</u>' (Exodus 40: 34).

'Indeed it came to pass, when the trumpeters and singers were as one, to make one sound to be heard in praising and thanking the Lord, and when they lifted up their voice with the trumpets and cymbals and instruments of music, and praised the Lord, saying: "For He is good, for His mercy endures forever, that the house, the house of the Lord, was filled with a cloud, so that the priests could not continue ministering because of the cloud; <u>for the glory of the Lord filled the house of God</u>' (2 Chronicles 5: 13, 14).

Therefore, when Apostle John speaks about Christ as the tabernacle which is filled with the glory of God and where the fullness of the Godhead (the Word) dwells, he is actually linking the two pictures of the Old and New Testaments.

The old picture of the tabernacle and the temple was a symbol and a reference to the new picture which became clear and manifested in Christ, the New

Tabernacle or the New Temple where the fullness of the Godhead dwells. He also *dwells in us* because Apostle John clearly states that *He tabernacled in us.*

This is exactly what Apostle Paul later said in Colossians:

'For in Him dwells all the fullness of the Godhead bodily; and you are complete in Him, who is the head of all principality and power' (Colossians 2: 9, 10).

These words highlight the human nature of Christ as the tabernacle or the temple.

This also occurs in the gospel of John, chapter 2, where he says:

'So the Jews answered and said to Him, "What sign do You show to us, since You do these things?" Jesus answered and said to them, "Destroy this temple, and in three days I will raise it up." Then the Jews said, "It has taken forty-six years to build this temple, and will You raise it up in three days?" <u>But He was speaking of the temple of His body</u>. Therefore, when He had risen from the dead, His disciples remembered that He had said this to them; and they believed the Scripture and the word which Jesus had said' (John 2: 18 – 22).

Apostle John who speaks about the importance of worship is spirit and truth and that the Father seeks those who worship Him, presents to us *the possibility of doing so in the Person of Christ* who was revealed and manifested as **the Word (the divine nature)** and **the Temple (the human nature).**

Yet, the Apostle also tells us that this manifestation of Christ as the Temple in whom dwells all the fullness of the Godhead (the divinity) and the glory, **desires also to dwell in us**.

This is highlighted by both Apostle John and Apostle Paul.

Apostle John writes the following words spoken by Jesus Himself:

'Jesus answered and said to him, "If anyone loves Me, he will keep My word; and My Father will love him, and We will come to him and make Our home with him' (John 14: 23).

Apostle Paul also highlights the same matter using the word *'temple'* where he wrote:

'Do you not know that you are the temple of God and that the Spirit of God dwells in you?' (1 Corinthians 3: 16)

The Apostle then continues to say:

'Or do you not know that your body is the temple of the

Holy Spirit who is in you, whom you have from God, and you are not your own?' (1 Corinthians 6: 19)

- **What does this mean practically?**

1. **Understanding what Christ has done for our sake; and then, accepting and receiving this divine work in us:**

Christ has filled His temple (His human nature) with His divine nature. This divine nature overcomes all the death, the decay and the mortality (resulting from sin) in that human nature.

This is the divine economy (oikonomia) of salvation!

First, Christ sanctified the human nature (which He took from us) in His Person, His Hypostasis; so that He may give it back to us as a holy sanctified nature that overcomes sin, weakness, and death.

This is what Apostle John meant when he wrote: *'And for their sakes I sanctify Myself, that they also may be sanctified by the truth'* (John 17: 19).

How can this be possible? How is it possible for Christ, who is holy by nature, to be sanctified?

The answer lies in the divine oikonomia. Christ assumes the human nature and sanctifies that nature so that He might first restore it in Himself and through Himself restore it to that beauty that it had in the beginning.

Through this sanctification, Christ bestowed His own attributes upon the human nature.

Christ's High-Priestly prayer in John 17 (where the above verse is mentioned) is not only intended for His disciples' sanctification, but it is also offered on behalf of all who would believe in Him in every subsequent age.

It is a universal gift and it is intended for all, because this sanctification in the Spirit is the means of re-establishing the lost communion with God.

2. Our responsibility

Therefore, our responsibility is to understand this matter so that we can unite with Christ and His life would flow in us.

Whoever communes with Christ, receives what Christ has done for us. Therefore, Apostle John presents the picture of the Vine and the branches (John 15:1-8) highlighting that we need the Spirit and the love of Christ to flow in us. We will be joined to Him like branches are joined to the vine. When we are attached by our love for Him, our hearts will be nourished by the streams of the Spirit, Christ's Spirit: *'Now if anyone does not have the Spirit of Christ, he is not His'* (Romans 8: 9b).

In order for this unity to take place and the Spirit of Christ and His presence to flow in us, we practically need the following:

- ○ To set our minds above the pleasures of the flesh in order to keep the beauty of the image that is implanted in us, unmarred and undistorted.

- ○ To live a sacrificial life because Christ has offered His life as a sacrifice for us: *'For even the Son of Man did not come to be served, but to serve, and to give His life a ransom for many'* (Mark 10: 45).

- ○ To search our heart (its disposition), to strive to have a pure heart [*'blessed are the pure in heart, for they shall see God'* (Matthew 5: 8)] and to live a virtuous life with correct doctrine.

3. **We need to pay attention to an important point regarding the new commandment that Jesus gave to His disciples**

'A new commandment I give to you, that you love one another; <u>as I have loved you</u>, that you also love one another. By this all will know that you are My disciples, if you have love for one another' (John 13: 34, 35).

What does Jesus mean by saying *'a new commandment'*? Wasn't this commandment of love mentioned in the Old Testament?

In Deuteronomy 6: 5, it is written: *'you shall love the Lord your God with all your heart, with all your soul, and with all your strength'*. This is also similar to what Jesus said in his talks with those who asked him about the greatest commandment *'you shall love the Lord your God with all your heart, with all your soul, and with all your mind. This is the first and great commandment'* (Matthew 22: 37 – 39).

Yet, in His final talks to His disciples before the Cross, Jesus talks about the new commandant saying: *'as I have loved you, that you also love one another'.* This means that the new commandment is to raise the level or standard of our love to be like that of the love of Christ; in other words, to raise it to the level of laying one's life, sacrificing to the point of death, as we read in the following verse:

'This is My commandment, that you love one another as I have loved you. Greater love has no one than this,

than to lay down one's life for his friends' (John 15: 12, 13).

It is a radical and a new kind of love. It is a love uniquely revealed by Christ where the love of God and the neighbour is placed higher than the love of the self. This indeed requires the same self-sacrificial and self-emptying humility that was revealed to us in Christ's Incarnation.

Because of this, Apostle John writes: *'everyone who loves is born of God and knows God. He who does not love does not know God, for God is love'* (1 John 4: 7, 8). The Apostle continues saying: *'God is love, and he who abides in love abides in God, and God in him'* (1 John 4: 16b).

Apostle Paul highlights that this love is being poured in us by the Holy Spirit (Romans 5: 5). It is not a human ability nor is it human feelings or emotions; it is the gift of God in Christ which is poured in us, making us love to the point of death—as the martyrs and saints did.

In this context, Apostle John writes: *'And they overcame him by the blood of the Lamb and by the word of their testimony, and <u>they did not love their lives to the death'</u>* (Revelation 12: 11).

Fruits and results:

This worship life in spirit and truth, which God the Father seeks and requests of us and which has become available and possible through the work of the Son, has great results.

Some of these results are:

a. A deep understanding of the Scriptures and the divine mysteries

According to the early Church teaching, *the worship in spirit and truth* is an important principle in interpreting the biblical text and a key to understanding the revelation in the Scriptures. Understanding the divine mysteries is also so closely connected to the spiritual life and to prayer and worship.

The veil has been torn from top to bottom, as we read in Matthew 27: 51: *'Then, behold, the veil of the temple was torn in two from top to bottom; and the earth quaked, and the rocks were split'*; and also in Mark 15: 38: *'Then the veil of the temple was torn in two from top to bottom'*.

Since the veil has been torn, this means that the mysteries of God have now become available for us.

b. Attracting people to Christ and dispersing/dissipating the clouds and the darkness of the devil

True worship has the power to draw people to Christ and to introduce them into His life.

In this context, Apostle John presents the following well-known scene:

'After these things Jesus showed Himself again to the disciples at the Sea of Tiberias, and in this way He showed Himself: Simon Peter, Thomas called the Twin, Nathanael of Cana in Galilee, the sons of Zebedee, and two others of His disciples were together. Simon Peter said to them, "I am going fishing." They said to him, "We are going with you also." They went out and immediately got into the boat, and that night they caught nothing. But when the morning had now come, Jesus stood on the shore; yet the disciples did not know that it was Jesus. Then Jesus said to them, "Children, have you any food?" They answered Him, "No." And He said to them, "Cast the net on the right side of the boat, and you will find some." So they cast, and now they were not able to draw it in because of the multitude of fish' (John 21: 1 – 6).

The disciples were unable to draw any fish into their nets. They worked all night, but failed to catch anything before *the advent of Christ*, which is *symbolically* linked to their encounter with Christ at daybreak where the mist of the devil was dispersed and the true light (Christ) arose. Jesus asked for food, since as God He hungers for the salvation of all!

c. The glory of God was granted to man and extended to the whole Creation because man is the head and the priest of Creation

We read about this in the intercessory prayer of Jesus where He prays: *'and the glory which You gave Me I have given them'* (John 17: 22).

Through participation in the divine nature, real transformation is made possible.

Christians are no longer merely human beings, but rather *'children of God'* and *'heavenly people'* since they have become partakers of the divine nature.[34]

o The glory of God is given to all without any distinction:

In his writings about *'worship in spirit and truth'*, St. Cyril never differentiated between clergy and laity because what Christ has made available, He has made available to every true worshipper no matter who he or she is.

---

34 Fifty Homilies -XVI, 8

Every person is granted the opportunity not only to be saved from the torment of eternal separation from God, but also to have the indescribable blessings of being eternally united to God, where God dwells within us and we become His temples.

As a result, divided humanity becomes united into one, with God and with one another.

The entire created world becomes God's temple —as a hymn of praise is offered to Him with one heart and one mind by brothers and sisters dwelling together in unity.

Appendix 1:

Biblical Study About 'the Covenant'

We first read about the *'covenant'* in God's words to Noah after he came out of the ark. The Lord said to Noah: *'And as for Me, behold, <u>I establish My covenant</u> <u>with you</u> and with your descendants after you'* (Genesis 9: 9).

The next time we read about the covenant is in Genesis 15 and 17, the well-known covenant which God established with Abraham.

What about Adam? Was there a covenant between God and Adam?

In fact, there is no reference to this in the Bible

and probably the reason for this is that Adam's relationship with God was direct and spontaneous; there was nothing to hinder it. However, after Adam's fall, hindrances to this relationship occurred: an internal hindrance (sin) and an external hindrance (the enemy). It; therefore, became necessary to have a certain form that would secure this relationship. This form was: *'establishing a covenant between God and man'.*

When humanity became corrupted with evil in the days of Noah, God sent the flood to wash the land and destroy the corrupted creation. Then, a new descendant started from a righteous man, Noah, whom the Bible describes saying: *'Noah was a just man, perfect in his generations. Noah walked with God'* (Genesis 6: 9).

Noah's family, consisting of 8 people, were the only people who entered the ark and witnessed the enormity of the judgment. The flood was dreadful. The Bible describes it saying: *'all the fountains of the great deep were broken up, and the windows of heaven were opened'* (Genesis 7:11). The Bible then continues to describe it saying: *'so He destroyed all living things which were on the face of the ground: both man and cattle, creeping thing and bird of the air. They were destroyed from the earth'* (Genesis 7:23).

This scene was a warning of how dreadful the judgment could be. Each one of Noah's family must have been reminding himself that if God became angry with them for some reason, He could make them all die in the same way.

Here we see the greatness of the *divine mercy and love*. God spoke with Noah saying:

'And as for Me, behold, I establish My covenant with you and with your descendants after you, and with every living creature that is with you: the birds, the cattle, and every beast of the earth with you, of all that go out of the ark, every beast of the earth. Thus I establish My covenant with you: Never again shall all flesh be cut off by the waters of the flood; <u>never again shall there be a flood to destroy the earth</u>*." And God said: "This is* <u>the sign of the covenant</u> *which I make between Me and you, and every living creature that is with you, for perpetual generations: I set My rainbow in the cloud, and it shall be for the sign of the covenant between Me and the earth. It shall be, when I bring a cloud over the earth, that the rainbow shall be seen in the cloud; and I will remember My covenant which is between Me and you and every living creature of all flesh; the waters shall never again become a flood to destroy all flesh. The rainbow shall be in the cloud, and I will look on it to remember* <u>the everlasting covenant</u> *between*

God and every living creature of all flesh that is on the earth." And God said to Noah, "This is the sign of the covenant which I have established between Me and all flesh that is on the earth' (Genesis 9: 9 – 17).

By this, God established the first covenant with man.

In this covenant, we notice the following:

- This covenant shows that God is a God of love, comfort, peace and security.

- This divine plan of *establishing a covenant* became the means of securing relationships between human beings afterwards.

- God has put upon Himself stipulations; yet, He did not require any conditions from the other party in the covenant.

- God made *'a sign'* for the covenant (a rainbow in the cloud).

When Noah's descendants multiplied and filled the earth, evil started to appear again.

We read about Nimrod, the descendant of Ham. The Bible says that: *'He was a mighty hunter before the Lord'* (Genesis 10: 9). In the original language, the phrase *'before the Lord'* means *'against the Lord'.*

We also read about the Tower of Babel (Genesis 11) and the human planning which was against God. The people were afraid and they attempted to find solutions that could protect them from the flood; they behaved as though they did not believe or trust the covenant between God and Noah; they were unwilling to establish a relationship of love and trust with God. Therefore, God confused their tongues and nullified their project. It is clear that the descendants of Noah were not happy to continue with the covenant made between God and their father, Noah.

Despite man's opposition and resistance, God adhered to His covenant and He did not destroy the earth as He had promised. Yet, He was sad because He is a God of love and He wants to keep His relationship with Man.

God thus searched and found a righteous man and a friend, Abraham, with whom He could establish another covenant. God chose Abraham and blessed him (Isaiah 51: 2; Genesis 12: 1 – 3).

God established two covenants with Abraham. One of them is mentioned in Genesis 15 and the other in Genesis 17.

What is the difference between these two covenants?

a. The first covenant with Abraham (Genesis 15: 18)

'On the same day the Lord made a covenant with Abram' (Genesis 15: 18).

This covenant was made because Abraham was going through a faith crisis. Abraham said to God: *'what will You give me, seeing I go childless, and the heir of my house is Eliezer of Damascus?'* (Genesis 15: 2)

Despite God's promise to Abraham that he will have a blessed descendant (in Genesis 12: 2, 3: *'I will make you a great nation...and in you all the families of the earth shall be blessed'*), Abraham started to doubt. Therefore, God made this first covenant with Abraham. Here, we see that the covenant was established to secure the relationship between God and man—because of the inner sin of doubt and the enemy's whispers trying to make man doubt God.

Here, we also witness a different method for establishing the covenant, different from the one used with Noah. God asked Abraham to offer sacrifices and cut them into halves and wait for Him. In fact, this was exactly the manner that the people (the surrounding tribes at the time of Abraham) used in making covenants between one another. They used to offer a sacrifice and part it into two halves and then walk to and fro between the two halves as a sign of an agreement between them; whoever contradicts this agreement/covenant exposes oneself to death. God asked Abraham to do exactly the same; and then God passed between the pieces of the sacrifices in the form of *'a smoking oven and a burning torch'* because God is fire:

'And it came to pass, when the sun went down and it was dark, that behold, there appeared a smoking oven and a burning torch that passed between those pieces' (Genesis 15: 17).

As a party in the covenant, God passed between the pieces of the sacrifices; His fire was illuminating (*'burning torch'*) to signify that He will illuminate the way of Abraham and his descendants whenever the darkness of the evil one comes upon them.

Abraham offered the sacrifices and then the vultures came and Abraham battled against them (verse11). This is the first time we see God teaching man (through Abraham) to fight *the fight of faith*. This reflects man's responsibility in the covenant. Since Abraham's battle was a battle of faith, his battle was with the vultures. The vultures refer to his war against the thoughts of doubt.

The word *'covenant'* is *'berith'* in Hebrew and it means *'cutting'*; this is derived from the concept of cutting the sacrifices and walking between them.

b. The second covenant with Abraham (Genesis 17)

Here, we witness another covenant and we notice that the time span between the first and second covenants was 13 years. Abraham was 86 years old (Genesis 16: 16) at the time of the first covenant and he was 99 years old (Genesis 17: 1) at the time of the second covenant. This period between the two covenants was given to Abraham to grow in the new faith which he received after he completed the battle with the vultures; the coming of the fire of the Lord; and the covenant that God established with him.

Similarly, God grants us certain periods of time at certain stages for the growth of our faith.

When Abraham's faith grew, God came to him to establish another covenant: *'I will make My covenant between Me and you, and will multiply you exceedingly'* (Genesis 17: 2).

Notice the following about this second covenant:

The first covenant was with *Abram* and it was related to *the land;* while this second covenant is related to granting Abraham *descendants*, which is a greater matter.

Also, his name changed from *'Abram'* to *'Abraham'* which means *'a father of nations';* signifying *'blessing'.*

God included Abraham's wife, Sarah, in this blessing (Genesis 17: 15) because the matter is related to having descendants; and so, both Abraham and his wife had to partake in this blessing.

A certain commitment was required as a sign of the covenant and that was: *'circumcision'.* *'Circumcision'* had a certain important significance that was revealed and unfolded throughout the generations and reached its fullness in the New Testament.

There was also a condition for the covenant and this was: *'walk before Me and be blameless'.*

In this verse (verse 1), we notice that the Scriptures use God's name, *'El Shaddai'*:

'I am El Shaddai; walk before Me, and be blameless' (Genesis 17: 1 –OJB).

This signifies that God (El Shaddai) grants man the ability to walk righteously with God.

In fact, 'El Shaddai' in the Hebrew language has two meanings. Firstly, it refers to the breast of a mother. A mother supports, enables and embraces. So, it refers to God who completely nourishes, satisfies, and supplies His people with all their needs as a mother would her child. It also means mountain indicating strength; and it means *'irresistible and unchanging'*.

Therefore, the word is used in this verse, in this context, to support the request that God made from Abraham asking him to walk righteously. As if God is telling Abraham: I am El Shaddai; I will embrace you, support you, and grant you the ability to walk righteously. At the same time God wants to say that His covenant with Abraham will be very strong, like a mountain; it is irresistible and unchanging.

Therefore, the surety (the guarantee) of the covenant is also highlighted in verse 1 where God is described as the *'Almighty God', 'El Shaddai'*; signifying that the covenant is secure, sure and guaranteed and no one (neither the enemy nor circumstances) can spoil it.

The privileges of the covenant: *'I will multiply*

you exceedingly...I will make you exceedingly fruitful' (Genesis 17: 2, 6); God's blessing.

The responsibilities of the covenant: *'in you all the families of earth shall be blessed'* (Genesis 12: 3).

This covenant became a covenant with all Abraham's descendants when they became one people, God's people, Israel.

God made a covenant with them in Mount Sinai:

'Now therefore, if you will indeed obey My voice and keep My covenant, then you shall be a special treasure to Me above all people; for all the earth is Mine. And you shall be to Me a kingdom of priests and a holy nation' (Exodus 19: 5, 6).

God had set for them *'the controls'* of the covenant which were *'the commandments'*; yet, they neglected them. After their exodus from Egypt, they broke the commandments and lost their obedience to God and their faith in God. Thus, they fell in the wilderness, and a complete generation died due to lack of obedience and lack of faith. Before entering the Land of Promise, God renewed the covenant with them:

'These are the words of the covenant which the Lord commanded Moses to make with the children of Israel in the land of Moab, besides the covenant which He made

with them in Horeb (Mount Sinai)' (Deuteronomy 29: 1).

The prophets then came and informed us that God intends to establish a *new covenant* because the fathers broke the first covenant:

'Behold, the days are coming, says the Lord, when I will make a <u>new covenant</u> with the house of Israel and with the house of Judah—not according to the covenant that I made with their fathers in the day that I took them by the hand to lead them out of the land of Egypt, <u>My covenant which they broke</u>, though I was a husband to them, says the Lord. But this is the covenant that I will make with the house of Israel after those days, says the Lord: I will put My law in their minds, and write it on their hearts; and I will be their God, and they shall be My people. No more shall every man teach his neighbour, and every man his brother, saying, 'Know the Lord,' for they all shall know Me, from the least of them to the greatest of them, says the Lord. For I will forgive their iniquity, and their sin I will remember no more' (Jeremiah 31: 31 – 34).

This is a clear reference to the New Testament and the Person of Jesus (as the true Israelite) with whom God will establish the covenant—which the fathers of Israel had broken in the old days. Jesus came as the true faithful Israelite. God, the Father, made His covenant with Jesus because Jesus is the New Adam who shall become the Head of a new descendant.

'Therefore, just as through one man sin entered the world, and death through sin, and thus death spread to all men, because all sinned' (Romans 5: 12).

'For if by the one man's offense many died, much more the grace of God and the gift by the grace of the one Man, Jesus Christ abounded to many' (Romans 5: 15).

'For as by one man's disobedience (Adam) *many were made sinners, so also by one Man's obedience many will be made righteous'* (Romans 5: 19).

Thus we can see that the Father made a covenant with His Son, Jesus; and through Jesus with us.

Some features of this new covenant

'By so much more Jesus has become a surety of a better covenant' (Hebrews 7: 22).

'But now He has obtained a more excellent ministry, inasmuch as He is also Mediator of a better covenant, which was established on better promises' (Hebrews 8: 6).

'He says: "Behold, the days are coming, says the Lord, when I will make a new covenant with the house of Israel and with the house of Judah—not according

to the covenant that I made with their fathers in the day when I took them by the hand to lead them out of the land of Egypt; because they did not continue in My covenant, and I disregarded them, says the Lord. For this is the covenant that I will make with the house of Israel after those days, says the Lord: I will put My laws in their mind and write them on their hearts; and I will be their God, and they shall be My people. None of them shall teach his neighbour, and none his brother, saying, 'Know the Lord,' for all shall know Me, from the least of them to the greatest of them. For I will be merciful to their unrighteousness, and their sins and their lawless deeds I will remember no more' (Hebrews 8: 7 – 12).

It is clear that *'establishing a covenant between God and man'* is an unchanging idea in God's mind; it directs humanity towards God's holy and blessed purposes.

We also notice that God's promise of blessing to Abraham remains as it is; yet, in the New Testament, it is fulfilled in Jesus Christ:

'You are sons of the prophets, and <u>of the covenant</u> which God made with our fathers, saying to Abraham, 'and in your seed all the families of the earth shall be blessed'. To you first, God, having raised up His Servant Jesus, sent Him to bless you, in turning away every one of you from your iniquities' (Acts 3: 25, 26).

'For the promise that he would be the heir of the world was not to Abraham or to his seed through the law, but through the righteousness of faith' (Romans 4: 13).

'Therefore it is of faith that it might be according to grace, so that the promise might be sure to all the seed, not only to those who are of the law, but also to those who are of the faith of Abraham, who is the father of us all' (Romans 4: 16).

'...that <u>the blessing of Abraham</u> might come upon the Gentiles in Christ Jesus, that we might receive the promise of the Spirit through faith' (Galatians 3: 14).

The above verses highlight the following

God's promise of blessing to Abraham remains as it is and it has been granted to us, to those who believe in Christ; being members implanted in His body (1Corinthians 12: 13) because it is written: *'has blessed us with every spiritual blessing in the heavenly places in Christ'* (Ephesians 1: 3).

We also understand **the first picture of the practical manifestation of the blessing** and that is: *'restoring man from his iniquities'*. It is the passive part of the blessing which is: removing the blockage.

The **advantages of the new covenant** are also so apparent. In Hebrews 8: 10 it is described as *'a better* covenant, which was established on better promises'. This is because the commandments became written on the hearts (Hebrews 8: 10) and we obey them by the power of the Holy Spirit through our fellowship with Him:

'For this is the covenant that I will make with the house of Israel after those days, says the Lord: I will put My laws in their mind and <u>write them on their hearts</u>; and I will be their God, and they shall be My people' (Hebrews 8: 10).

'For the law of the Spirit of life in Christ Jesus has made me free from the law of sin and death. For what the law could not do in that it was weak through the flesh, God did by sending His own Son in the likeness of sinful flesh, on account of sin: He condemned sin in the flesh, that the righteous requirement of the law might be fulfilled in us who do not walk according to the flesh but according to the Spirit' (Romans 8: 2 – 4).

'The grace of the Lord Jesus Christ, and the love of God, and the communion of the Holy Spirit be with you all. Amen' (2 Corinthians 13: 14).

Christ is the surety of the covenant and the living hope which is an anchor for the soul, the anchor of hope which we hold onto.

'By so much more Jesus has become a surety of a better

covenant' (Hebrews 7: 22).

'That by two immutable (unchangeable) *things, in which it is impossible for God to lie; we might have strong consolation, who have fled for refuge to lay hold of the hope set before us. This hope we have as an anchor of the soul, both sure and steadfast, and which enters the Presence behind the veil, where the forerunner has entered for us, even Jesus, having become High Priest forever according to the order of Melchizedek'* (Hebrews 6: 18 – 20).

Thus, we can say:

○ It is so important to understand the truth of the divine revelation about the covenant from the very beginning, from the time of Noah, until Jesus because we are now parties in this covenant.

○ After receiving this revelatory understanding, it is important to believe the divine revelation and practise a steadfast faith and living hope.

○ Then, we need to learn to keep the covenant constantly active and effective, especially in the practical daily life.

○ The condition of the covenant also remains the same as it was with Abraham; namely, *'walk before Me and be blameless'.* However, in the New Testament, the Holy Spirit –through the work of grace, enables us to do so.

o   We should not forget that in the Sermon on the Mount Jesus said: *'Therefore you shall be perfect, just as your Father in heaven is perfect'* (Matthew 5: 48). This echoes the Lord's words to Abraham.

This is practically achieved by:

A. *Spiritual diligence*

'By the Spirit you put to death the deeds of the body' (Romans 8: 13).

Refer also to Philippians 2: 12, 13; 1 Corinthians 9: 24 – 27; Hebrews 4: 11; 2 Peter 1: 4 – 11.

One needs to remind himself that he is now a partner of God Himself, the great covenant Partner. It is a great honour; but, also a great responsibility. One must be careful lest he bring shame to God's Great Name (Romans 2: 24).

Therefore, one needs to consider the following points:

i. The status

Is it possible for a great president or director of a company to be in partnership with a beggar, an immoral person or a thief? Of course, this can never happen because this would dishonour the company and spoil the whole thing. The same applies in God's partnership with us. We need to vigil on our inner state and status in this partnership.

ii. Fellowship leading to friendship

This demands *total surrender; total trust; and total reliance on God.*

This means that one has to live a life of *'sanctifying the present moment'* (John 5:19).

iii. Sacrificial life

In this respect, we need to remember the words of Jesus when he said:

'For even the Son of Man did not come to be served, but to serve, and to give His life a ransom for many' (Mark 10: 45).

'I beseech you therefore, brethren, by the mercies of God, that you present your bodies a living sacrifice, holy, acceptable to God, which is your reasonable service' (Romans 12: 1).

B. Submitting to God's chastening in dealing with the power of the fallen soul that hinders the work of the Spirit.

'You have not yet resisted to bloodshed, striving against sin. And you have forgotten the exhortation which speaks to you as to sons: "My son, do not despise the chastening of the Lord, nor be discouraged when you are rebuked by Him; For whom the Lord loves He chastens, and scourges every son whom He receives." If you endure chastening, God deals with you as with sons; for what son is there whom a father does not chasten? But if you are without chastening, of which all have become partakers, then you are illegitimate and not sons. Furthermore, we have had human fathers who corrected us, and we paid them respect. Shall we not much more readily be in subjection to the Father of spirits and live? For they indeed for a few days chastened us as seemed best to them, but He for our profit, that we may be partakers of His holiness. Now no chastening seems to be joyful for the present, but painful; nevertheless, afterward it yields the peaceable fruit of righteousness to those who have been trained by it' (Hebrews 12: 4 – 11).

God had actually used this method of divine chastening with all His great men:

- o **Job** suffered many afflictions; yet, he continued

to trust God and exercise faith.

○ **Abraham** came out of his land and became a sojourner; famine struck and he went to Egypt where his wife was taken and was later returned; he was barren and bore the long tests of faith.

○ **Jacob** faced many difficulties with his two wives and with Laban; his wife, Rachel, died; and he lost his son, Joseph.

○ **Joseph** was sold by his brothers; was falsely accused by the wife of Potiphar; and went to prison.

○ **Moses** had to flee to Midian and went through a long period of training in the wilderness –for 40 years.

○ **David** was chased by Saul and had to hide in caves for many years; he suffered the trial of his son, Absalom, and the trial towards the end of his life when his love to God became lukewarm.

C. *Activating the sign of the covenant*

God talks clearly about the sign of the New Covenant which is *'baptism'*; it is equivalent to *'circumcision'.*

'In Him you were also circumcised with the circumcision made without hands, by putting off the body of the sins of the flesh, by the circumcision of Christ, buried with Him in baptism, in which you also were raised with Him through faith in the working of God, who raised Him from the dead' (Colossians 2: 11, 12).

Baptism is a spiritual circumcision and it is the sign of the New Testament:

'For he is not a Jew who is one outwardly, nor is circumcision that which is outward in the flesh; but he is a Jew who is one inwardly; and <u>circumcision is that of the heart, in the Spirit,</u> not in the letter; whose praise is not from men but from God' (Romans 2: 28, 29).

Thus, we are called for the circumcision of the heart by the Spirit.

What kind of circumcision is this?

It is cutting off the foreskin that is formed on the heart. The circumcision of the heart by the Spirit requires the continuous work of the Holy Spirit. It is the renewed act of baptism because baptism is a covenant (the sign of the new covenant); baptism is death and resurrection with Christ.

'Or do you not know that as many of us as were baptized into Christ Jesus were baptized into His death?

Therefore we were buried with Him through baptism into death, that just as Christ was raised from the dead by the glory of the Father, even so we also should walk in newness of life. For if we have been united together in the likeness of His death, certainly we also shall be in the likeness of His resurrection' (Romans 6: 3 – 5).

Let us pause and ponder:

+ The above important biblical truths are, unfortunately, usually taken for granted. We consider that they were fulfilled when we believed in Christ and that there is nothing else to be done. However, because they transfer to us a spiritual power that drives us forward, we need this power to be continually renewed inside us by the work of Holy Spirit. In such a way, the circumcision of the heart by the Spirit becomes always active and effective. This in turn makes the covenant between us and God always active; and hence, we can reap the fruits of the covenant and its blessings; and they become apparent in our lives.

+ The blessing of the covenant is: *to cause clear and extended blessing,* as God told Abraham: *'in you all the families of earth shall be blessed'.*

+ This was God's promise to Abraham and it was fulfilled in Christ. This should also extend through each one of us as the body of Christ, the Church.

+ Yet, why don't we see this happening with every believer—each in his place, time and spheres of authority? God has made us kings; God promised Abraham to have authority on earth. This was a restoration of Adam's authority on earth which Adam had lost, but it had to be restored. This does not happen because the covenant is not active; the sign of the covenant is hindered. God's covenant is the same since Abraham, as discussed above. It became re-established in Christ; and hence, the sign of the covenant is also the same. It is circumcision, not in the flesh but in the heart as Apostle Paul says in Romans 2.

Why is the sign of the covenant hindered (and so the covenant is not fully effective)?

This is because the heart can become uncircumcised; it can become surrounded with foreskin.

The foreskin is formed on the heart due to the activity of the fallen nature that requires the continuous act of the cross by the Holy Spirit. It is our responsibility to release this through spiritual diligence. The foreskin can also be formed due to external trials and temptations from the world and the devil to which the fallen nature inside us responds.

As a result, the foreskin is weaved on the heart; and consequently hinders the effectiveness of the life of the Spirit.

This foreskin is dealt with through the above mentioned economies; namely, the economy of spiritual diligence, the economy of the divine chastening, and the activation of the sign of the covenant. These economies break the power of the fallen soul. The fallen nature can sometimes be deceived by the enemy; this allows the foreskin of corruption to enter us from the world and cover the heart again.

The divine chastening together with the spiritual diligence sanctify the soul and make the heart tender (the tenderness of the heart: 2 Chronicles 34: 27), like David's heart (1 Samuel 24: 5; 2 Samuel 24: 10), instead of the hardened heart due to self-centeredness.

Blessing the whole creation

Being priests on behalf of the whole creation, the early fathers realised their spiritual responsibility to bless all creation. Therefore, they used to offer praises of thanksgiving to God every day (Psalm 136) and proclaim the blessing on all creation by providing creation with a mouth that blesses God—through the mouth of the worshippers who stood up in the very early hours of every morning to proclaim the praise of all creation to God the Lord.

For example, they would praise saying:

"Bless the Lord, O, you works of the Lord.

Praise Him and exalt Him above all forever.

Bless the Lord, O, you clouds and winds.

Praise Him and exalt Him above all forever."

(From the praises of the early Church, fourth century)

The early fathers became bearers of God's *blessing of priesthood*:

'The Lord bless you and keep you; the Lord make His face shine upon you, and be gracious to you; the Lord lift up His countenance upon you, and give you peace' (Numbers 6: 24 – 26).

They were keepers of their people; keepers of the blessings of the covenant. God keeps His people according to His promises:

'The Lord is your keeper; the Lord is your shade at your right hand' (Psalm 121: 5).

'The Lord will perfect that which concerns me; Your mercy, O the Lord, endures forever; do not forsake the works of Your hands' (Psalm138: 8).

'The Lord preserves the simple; I was brought low, and He saved me' (Psalm116: 6).

They also had holy zeal for all what is related to the Lord and His Kingdom. They continually interceded for the extension of the Kingdom of God.

Because their life was full of light due to the presence and dwelling of God in them (John 14: 23; Ephesians 3: 17), they attracted others to the faith, the faith in Jesus Christ. Their lives became a testimony (an incarnated message) that testified for their words. They lived a life similar to the life of the apostles of the first Church:

'And with great power the apostles gave witness to the resurrection of the Lord Jesus. And great grace was upon them all' (Acts 4: 33).

The work of God with them and the accompaniment of Jesus according to His promise to them were so apparent:

'And they went out and preached everywhere, the Lord working with them and confirming the word through the accompanying signs' (Mark 16: 20).

Appendix 2:

A Study in Psalm 119

Introduction

According to documented reports from the early centuries, this Psalm was prayed daily by many worshippers, especially at midnight. It is still being prayed by many worshippers and believers today as well.

This Psalm reveals important dimensions in God's Word. It highlights how this worshiping psalmist saw God's Word from many angles.

The Psalm is arranged according to the Hebrew

alphabets: every stanza (passage) of the 22 stanzas starts with one of the Hebrew letters in an alphabetic order. Each stanza consists of 8 verses and these 8 verses start with the same alphabet of that stanza.

According to scholars, there are at least 8 words which the Psalmist uses to describe the Word of God, the way he knew it and experienced it.

It is believed that David is the author of this Psalm. He probably wrote it after being anointed by Samuel, the prophet. But, it seems that it was written after some time of receiving this anointing because the inspiration of the Holy Spirit is clear in it; and also the Psalmist's advanced spiritual experiences are clear.

In studying this Psalm, we will look at two main points:

I.   Words which express the Psalmist's experience with the word of God (8 key words)

II.   Spiritual experiences from the life of this worshiping Psalmist (8 main principles)

I. Words which express the Psalmist's experience with the word of God and some spiritual comments on them:

1. The law (Torah in Hebrew)

The word *'law'* occurs 25 times and it refers to the teaching which Moses received from the Lord in Sinai. The Psalmist truly loved the law of God and meditated on it. This word is mentioned in all the stanzas, except the second one.

2. Testimonies (Edoth)

These are related to God's testimony concerning Himself, His Person and His righteousness.

They are also related to God's testimony about *His will* which He reveals to man; so that the believers may follow it.

These testimonies also show the greatness of *God's love* for man and His good will towards man.

3. The statutes (Piqqudim) and the orders or commands

The word occurs 21 times. This shows how much

this worshipper loved God's statutes because he saw them through the eyes of God.

'*Statutes*' means commitment to a certain duty. God entrusts man with divine matters about Himself so that man can practise them; and so that through them, man may be protected from many evils and from the various deceptions of the evil one that aim at hindering him or even destroying his life.

We, as people of the New Testament, have treated this word with great reservation due to our ignorance of God's mind regarding it. We considered it a word that belongs to the 'law' of the Old Testament, a legalistic word; while in actual fact it is a word of worship; and every worshipper who loves the Word of God is able to enter into its divine mystery.

4. The wisdom (Chuqqim), verse 98, Beirut translation

This word is derived from a verb which means '*to engrave or to carve*'. This highlights that when the Word of God goes deep into a person's heart, it carves in the heart methods and principles that make the person wise. We also notice that all the artistic decorations of the temple were made by carving.

The landmarks of the spiritual road that are carved and engraved clearly—before us are the teachings handed down to us by the fathers and patriarchs; so that, we can follow in their footsteps and thus be protected from deceptions—whether they are deceptions from the self or from the evil one.

In the New Testament, Christ came as Wisdom for us from God. When He is formed in us (Galatians 4:19), He Himself becomes our wisdom in all we say or do (1 Corinthians 1: 30; 2:7).

5. The precepts (Mitsvot) or commandments

This word appears 22 times. It highlights how the Psalmist recognises God's authority and that God's precepts teach us to obey Him and submit to Him for our own good.

6. The ordinances (Misphatim) or judgments

This word occurred 23 times. It teaches us that God has put a constitution for man to live by and that God judges man's actions according to these ordinances.

Therefore, these ordinances show us God's

methods and goals in dealing with man from the beginning to the end. His wisdom and His goodness are revealed to us so that we are not offended by Him, but rather change our thoughts and ways in accordance to His thoughts and ways (Isaiah 55: 8, 9).

7. The word 'Dabar' and the sayings (Imrah) or promises

The word *'Dabar'* is mentioned 24 times and it indicates God's revelation to man.

The sayings (Imrah) occurs 19 times and it means the breath of God, God's utterance.

St. Augustine warns us about the way we turn the pages of the Bible, because he sees them as the swaddling clothes of the baby Jesus and baby Jesus being wrapped within them. This means that we will meet Him as we turn the pages of the Bible, if we do so with a heart open to the Spirit.

How marvellous it is to receive the breath of God anew while reading His word! It will dissipate our darkness; give us life; enlighten our souls and our minds; and keep death away from us.

8. The Way (Dereb) and the Truth/faithfulness (Orah)

The word the *'way'* appears 13 times; and the word the *'truth'* is mentioned 5 times.

These two words prophetically point to Christ who will come in the flesh for our salvation, that He is the only Way to the Father and He is the incarnate Truth who bears within Him the everlasting life for man.

II. Spiritual experiences from the life of this worshiping Psalmist

Since the figure 8 was used twice in this psalm regarding the number of verses in each stanza and also the Psalmist use of 8 words to express the way he knew and experienced the Word of God, it is appropriate to use this same arrangement and put the spiritual experiences of the Psalmist in 8 main principles.

1. Wholeheartedness

The Psalmist seeks God with all his heart: *'Blessed are those who keep his testimonies, who seek Him with their whole heart'* (from stanza 1 in the Agpya[35], or verse 2 according to the English translations); and also: *'I will keep Your precepts with my whole heart'* (stanza 9 in the Agpya or verse 69 in English translation).

He sees that keeping the commandments and precepts goes hand in hand with seeking God with the whole heart. This is because the commandments reveal what is in the heart and fix what is amiss within it, making it perfect.

He also sees that as the heart grows more and more in the path of perfection, it teaches the person to give thanks and praise in a better way; because it is a heart that is tuned to God's will (1st and 22nd stanza in the Agpya and verses 7 and 171 in English).

'I will praise You with uprightness of heart, when I learn Your righteous judgments' (verse 7).

'My lips shall utter praise, for You teach me Your statutes' (verse 171).

As a result, the heart offers worship for the pleasure of God; and as we read in Leviticus 1: 9, God desires a sweet aroma in our sacrifices of worship.

---

35 Agpya is the book of prayer in the Coptic Church

2. The Word of God keeps one from sinning
(stanza 2 and 22 in the Agpya, verses 11 and 176 in English)

'Your word I have hidden in my heart, that I might not sin against You' (verse 11).

'I have gone astray like a lost sheep; seek Your servant, for I do not forget Your commandments' (verse 176).

When we worship God using His word, the word dwells in us and the Holy Spirit reminds us of it. It is not only a light coming from the commandment, but it is also a divine preserving and helping power (John 14: 26; Hebrews 4: 12; Proverbs 6: 22, 23; Psalm 119: 105).

Because of this, we should never stop meditating on the word of God, chew on it, ruminate on it and murmur it, according to the Hebrew origin of the word *'meditate on'*. This will allow the word of God to dwell in us (Colossians 3:16) and we will become full with the spirit of the word, the Spirit of God. This will enable us to discern not only the good from the bad; but also the good, the better, and the best. We will acquire a deeper love for God and we will understand His mind and be drawn to Him. We will hate sin more and more as it will become so ugly in our eyes. As a result, we are set free from its power and we enter into deeper dimensions in the freedom of the Spirit.

The Psalmist amazes us by his knowledge, assurance and confidence that even if he loses the way, the Shepherd will seek him. This is because the commandment made a bond between them, a special mystical bond between the shepherd and the lost sheep. The dwelling of the commandment in the sheep makes the sheep restless until it goes back to be with the flock. It does not stop to groan till it is restored. On His part, the Shepherd cannot rest till He gets His lost sheep back because the sheep is bound to His heart with the mystical sacred bond of the commandment.

3. The hunger to go deep into the word of God: a hunger to experience the warmth of a closer relationship with God (3rd stanza in the Agpya, verses 18, 19, and 24 in English)

'Open my eyes, that I may see wondrous things from Your law. I am a stranger in the earth; do not hide Your commandments from me...Your testimonies also are my delight and my counsellors' (verses 18, 19, 24).

There is a special mystery about this psalmist. He

became a stranger, estranged from everybody, even his own folks. This is why it is very possible that this psalmist is David. It is also because of his faithful way in following the Lord and for the fact that he lived many years in caves and had to leave his parents in Moab (1 Samuel 22: 3). He found solace and strength in the word of God.

The Holy Scriptures with all the wonders and consolations in them became a family for him. So, instead of seeking a friend or a relative, especially when he faced a problem or felt lonely, he sought God in His word and found in Him a friend closer than his own folks (Proverbs 18: 24).

Not only this, but he also had a hunger to go deeper; he sought the depth of the word of God; and in it, he found solace and special warmth: *'I am a stranger in the earth; do not hide Your commandments from me* (verse 19).

He realised that the only source of help in his sojourning is the word of God. He realised that there are many mysteries hidden from the eye and they cannot be revealed by just a quick first reading; there is a need for persistent hunger and seeking God: *'Open my eyes, that I may see wondrous things from Your law'* (verse 18). These wonders satiate his hunger and provide him with help, comfort, and warmth.

Entering the depth of the word of God is like entering God's very presence where there is the true continual warmth!

4. Consolation in humiliation and sojourning, even when reaching the point of death (stanzas 4, 7, and 12 in the Agpya; verses 25, 28, 49, 50, 54, 92, and 93 in English)

It is evident that the Psalmist went through certain experiences that brought him to the point of death; yet, the word of God with all the promises, consolations, and the light it gives, helped him to find the way out and brought him back to life.

Thus, the word of God became for him an eternal memory: *'I will never forget Your precepts, for by them You have given me life* (verse 93).

'My soul clings to the dust; revive me according to Your word' (verse 25). These are the words of someone who is deeply afflicted to the point of death because whoever clings to the dust is like one entering the grave.

He was also even more afflicted and humiliated as a result of the various trials, the work of the evildoers, and the surrounding circumstances that distressed him. Yet, he regained his dignity and comfort through the word of God and its promises; he held fast unto them and they proved right.

In this way, he learned to hold unto the promises of God and find them realised and fulfilled for him: *'My soul melts from heaviness; strengthen me according to Your word'* (verse 28); *'Remember the word to Your servant, upon which You have caused me to hope. This is my comfort in my affliction, for Your word has given me life'* (verses 49, 50). He learned to wait for the Lord according to His promises: *'Your statutes have been my songs in the house of my pilgrimage'* (verse 54).

The word of God was his only consolation in his sojourning:

'Unless Your law had been my delight, I would then have perished in my affliction (verse 92).

5. God is righteous and His ways are good (stanzas 9, 10 in the Agpya, verses 67, 71, and 75 in English)

When he was afflicted, he was not resentful. He realised that these things happened to him because he was careless about certain things and because he had committed some mistakes or sins. Thus, for him, these experiences were a call to wake up and a warning coming to him from the Good and Faithful God.

If he had been resentful and had not seen these afflictions from this perspective and through this light, he would not have benefited from them and he could have stumbled and become offended by God. Yet, he said: *'Before I was afflicted I went astray, but now I keep Your word* (verse 67); and also: *'I know, O Lord, that Your judgments are right, and that in faithfulness You have afflicted me'* (verse 75). He testified to the righteousness, goodness, and truth of God by saying: *'in faithfulness You have afflicted me'*.

Not only this, but he also knew and experienced the fruits that result from such experiences –when they are accepted from the hand of the Lord with humility and in a positive way. He experienced how they become a source of mercy and comfort, and even a means of opening the heart and the spirit of the person to learn the things of God. And so, he said: *'It is good for me that I have been afflicted, that I may learn*

Your statutes (verse 71); and also: *'I know, O Lord, that Your judgments are right, and that in faithfulness You have afflicted me. Let, I pray, Your merciful kindness be for my comfort, according to Your word to Your servant. Let Your tender mercies come to me, that I may live; for Your law is my delight'* (verses 75 – 77).

6. The wisdom and understanding, the renewed infilling with the Spirit (stanza 13, 17 in the Agpya, verses 98 – 100, 130, 131 in English)

How did this worshiping Psalmist experience this degree of wisdom which surpassed that of the elders and the teachers! How did he even dare to say that he surpassed the teachers and the elders in wisdom and in understanding (while we surely know that he learned to be humble as a result of what he had gone through)!

The reason behind this is that the teachers gained their wisdom from studying and the elders gained it through the experiences of the many years; but, he received everything from above, not from any earthly resources. It was God's mind and wisdom. It was God's Spirit that taught him, as he worshipped God and meditated on His word all the day: *'Oh, how I love Your law! It is my meditation all the day!'* (Verse 97)

His spirit was stirred and his desires were set aflame; and so, he opened his mouth and panted after God and after His love—as the saints have done throughout all the ages. He knew how to draw and attract the Spirit of God: *'I opened my mouth and panted, for I longed for Your commandments'* (verse 131); and according to the translation in the Agpya: *'I opened my mouth and attracted a spirit for myself'*.

Because of this, the Church used this part in the rituals of ordaining priests and bishops. The bishop or the patriarch says this verse and blows in the mouth of the newly ordained person to give him a new infilling of the Spirit.

7. The holy zeal (stanza 16 in the Agpya; verses 126, 127 in English)

'It is time to work for the Lord, because they have broken your laws' (Agpya translation).

'It is time for You to act, O Lord, for they have regarded Your law as void (Verse 126, NKJV).

By continually meditating on the word of God, the Psalmist became very sensitive to all the things of God. As a result, he realised how others have left the path of God and have forsaken His law.

What was his response to this?

It was an amazing response; he was zealous for the Lord and he knew that he has to work more and call others to work too in order to restore the people to God and to His laws.

In response to the negligence happening around him, the Psalmist loved God's laws and commandments even more; he held unto them; prayed with them; and obeyed them.

If someone keeps God's commandments in their generation, this restores to the generation the authority of God and His word; and this in itself is accounted as a work of the Kingdom. This was the work of the worshippers and saints who lived in the deserts; they worshiped continually and meditated on the word of God; so that, the word of God would take its place in their generation. This was the movement of the Holy Spirit over those who were ready to receive Him at the time when God and His word were neglected and ignored and at the time when the spirit of the world crept in and took over. The history of the Church clearly reflects this both in the East and the West. Though people may not fully recognise this, heaven (God and His angels) knows it. The evil powers also see this work and are terrified by it because it limits their influence and causes their power over the people and nations to be broken.

Was not this David's position when he saw Goliath defying God and His people? He knew that it is time to work for the Lord because he was zealous for the Lord and wanted to show that God is great and could conquer this Philistine. Therefore, he used simple means, his sling and some smooth stones:

'Then David said to the Philistine, "You come to me with a sword, with a spear, and with a javelin. But I come to you in the name of the Lord of hosts, the God of the armies of Israel, whom you have defied. This day the Lord will deliver you into my hand, and I will strike you and take your head from you. And this day I will give the carcasses of the camp of the Philistines to the birds of the air and the wild beasts of the earth, that all the earth may know that there is a God in Israel. Then all this assembly shall know that the Lord does not save with sword and spear; for the battle is the Lord's, and He will give you into our hands' (1 Samuel 17: 45 – 47).

8. His experience with persecution and the persecutors (stanza 11, 20, 21 in the Agpya; verses 83 – 88, 153, 157, 161 in English)

He was not spared persecution. Actually, his suffering increased to the extent that he described himself as a *wineskin in ice* (Agpya) or *a wineskin in the smoke* (English). It is clear that the Hebrew word can mean both words. The trials he went through made him feel as if he was a wineskin cracking from being in the cold, the ice, or a wineskin that is burning by fire and the smoke suffocating him. Whether it is the suffering from severe cold or severe heat, it was severe suffering. In verse 87, he even described it as if it was his end: *'They almost made an end of me on earth'.*

He was persecuted; he suffered afflictions and humiliation from the leaders (princes), but the amazing thing is that he remembered God and quickly turned to His word; and so, he found the treasures of the conquerors and he forgot his suffering.

Through all his suffering, his consolation came from worship and from the word of God; his hope in God remained firm; and thus, he passed through suffering with success.

Because of the purity of his heart which resulted from worship and from loving and keeping the word of God, he did not even ask revenge for himself towards those evildoers.

List of References

Archimandrite Zacharias, *Christ: our Way and our life.*

Bishop Hilarion Alfeyev, *The Mystery of Faith.*

Cyril of Alexandria, *Adoration in Spirit.*

Lossky, *In the image and likeness of God.*

Lossky, *Mystical Theology of the Eastern Church.*

Lossky, *Orthodox Theology: An Introduction.*

Metropolitan Hierotheos, *I know a man in Christ.*

Staniloae, Dumitru, *The Experience of God.*

St. Macarius, *Fifty Homilies*, XVI.

St. Symeon, the new theologian, *Divine Eros.*

ALSO BY THE AUTHOR

Responsibility for the Generation

God's grace has been given to us for free so we have a responsibility to share this grace with others. Our responsibility toward this generation is greater because this is a generation of the end times, a time filled with global conflict and struggles. This book presents the necessary guidelines and spiritual principles that will enable us to realize our responsibility toward this generation, how to bless it and minister to it.

Prayers and Prophesying - Build Up Your Inner man

Learn how to pray and proclaim the blood of Jesus and prophesy through the verses of the Bible in order to develop and mature our inner spiritual man toward the purpose of the formation of Christ within us.

My Bridegroom Incarnated for Me

The book contains a series of messages for the children of God who desire to consecrate the Christmas season through prayer, worship and reading to the word of God in order to enter more deeply into the mystery of Christ's Incarnation.

The Kingdom of God and the End Times

How do we understand the Kingdom of God and the scene of the end times, biblically and practically? You will learn about the Kingdom of God and the world of today; its stages and aspects; the economy of the end times. You will also learn important economies about the kingdom of the Antichrist. You will learn how to resist the evil economies by the triumphing grace of God. This book offers an understanding of the Holy Spirit's counter economies that preserves the Church so that she would complete her mission as the prepared Bride awaiting His return!

The Bride & the End Times

Learn about the Bride of Christ, the Church, and the special divine economy of the end times in relation to the Bride. Is the term, 'the Bride', exclusive to the New Testament? Who will be the Bride of Christ in the end times and what is her commission? Where do the Jews fit in the divine economy? What is the divine economy for our days? How can we practically live as a Bride of Christ? The book also discusses the different stages of the divine economy, starting from the beginning to the present time. It also sheds light on the economy of this era of the end times. You will also learn the importance of restoring our lost spiritual inheritance and ideas about the scene of the second coming of Christ.

The Inner Man & the Formation of Christ

This book will help you find your way out of spiritual limitations and struggles to enter into the unsearchable riches in Christ. It will take you step by step into the biblical revelation about the 'inner man' and 'being transformed into Christ-likeness'. In this book you will also find answers and explanations to questions like: What is the 'inner man', according to the biblical revelation? What are the different stages of spiritual growth? Is there a link between the spiritual growth and the 'inner man'? How is this all related to the formation of Christ in us; and how does this formation take place? The book provides a discussion of the principles of the formation of Christ within us and their practical application as tools that help build our inner man. The purpose of this book is to help you find true release in your spiritual life, build your inner spiritual life, and enter into the unsearchable riches that have been granted to us in Christ.

All books are available on Amazon.com